The World According to Cunk

Also by Philomena Cunk

Cunk on Everything

The World According to Cunk

An Illustrated History of All World Events Ever*
*Space Permitting

PHILOMENA CUNK

GRAND CENTRAL

New York Boston

Copyright © 2024 by House of Tomorrow Ltd., Charlie Brooker,
Ben Caudell, Jason Hazeley, and Joel Morris

Cover copyright © 2024 by Hachette Book Group, Inc.

Hachette Book Group supports the right to free expression and the value of copyright. The purpose of copyright is to encourage writers and artists to produce the creative works that enrich our culture.

The scanning, uploading, and distribution of this book without permission is a theft of the author's intellectual property. If you would like permission to use material from the book (other than for review purposes), please contact permissions@hbgusa.com. Thank you for your support of the author's rights.

Grand Central Publishing
Hachette Book Group
1290 Avenue of the Americas, New York, NY 10104
grandcentralpublishing.com
@grandcentralpub

Published in Great Britain in 2024 by John Murray Press
First U.S. Hardcover Edition: November 2024

Grand Central Publishing is a division of Hachette Book Group, Inc. The Grand Central Publishing name and logo is a registered trademark of Hachette Book Group, Inc.

The publisher is not responsible for websites (or their content) that are not owned by the publisher.

The Hachette Speakers Bureau provides a wide range of authors for speaking events. To find out more, go to hachettespeakersbureau.com or email HachetteSpeakers@hbgusa.com.

Grand Central Publishing books may be purchased in bulk for business, educational, or promotional use. For information, please contact your local bookseller or the Hachette Book Group Special Markets Department at special.markets@hbgusa.com.

Illustrations copyright © 2024 by Diane Morgan. Netflix logo © 2024 by Netflix.

Print book interior design by Craig Burgess

Library of Congress Cataloging-in-Publication Data has been applied for.

ISBNs: 978-1-5387-7382-6 (hardcover), 978-1-5387-7384-0 (ebook)

Printed in the United States of America

LSC-C

Printing 2, 2024

To Paul, my mate

Contents

Introduction   1

1. The First Chapter   6
2. Chapter Two   36
3. The Third Chapter   62
4. The Enlightenedment   84
5. The Fifth Chapter   96
6. Britain Rues the Waves   112
7. Gone West!   132
8. World Wars 1–2 Inclusive   144
9. The Post-War Twentieth Century   168
10. The Global Globe   206

    Index   245

Introduction

by Philomena Cunk
(like the rest of the book too)

Yuval Noah Harari's done it. Niall Ferguson's done it. A. J. P. Taylor's done it. Simon Schama loves doing it, and says he does it as often as he can. Today, even some women have done it, and many claim to enjoy it. And now, I'm doing it too. It sounds like I'm talking about sex, because sex sells, apparently, in a way that non-fiction doesn't; but I'm actually talking about what you have in your hands: A Landmark Complete Shorter History of the World. Nothing left out, everything left in, and yet slim enough to slip into your pocket to read at a boring wedding where you're sitting on the randoms' table without a plus one. It's the most comprehensive history of the world ever – until a new war happens, in which case you will have to write that in yourself.

    I'm Philomena Cunk, Britain's foremost documentarian, thinkerer, and now, book-grower. You'll have seen me on such shows as *Cunk on Britain, Cunk on Earth, Cunk's Quest For Meaning*, and an as-yet-unbroadcast episode of *Celebrity Bake-Off* where I make a lemon drizzle cake that doesn't quite go to plan, accompanied by plinky-plonk incidental music.

When the publisher of this book (forget her name and I've lost her email now, Kate someone?) asked me to write a book about The Complete History of Civilisation on Earth, it didn't take me long to say, no thanks, that would take ages.

No, she said, it only needs to be 50,000 words. Nobody wants long books. Especially when there's so many great TikToks to watch; these days a book is really only a thing you buy for Christmas for someone you don't know well enough to buy a proper present, but you remember mentioning they had a vague interest in something that's in it. And a book about *everything that has happened on earth* is going to appeal to a lot of people. Especially if we can translate it into different languages and get the price point right. And put a picture of you on the front, because you've been on Netflix. So you're probably reading this book now because someone somewhere who doesn't know you very well thinks you're a fan of the Byzantines, or the Vandals, or the Ancient Sumerians. Or, let's face it, a fan of me.

In this important and yet pleasingly concise and manageable book, I'll be going on a journey (only metaphorically; most of it was written in an independent coffee shop on the Ball's Pond Road) to look at what people in the past did to make life on the planet bearable in the present, but unfortunately also unsustainable in the future.

It's a journey (again, actually I'm going nowhere; I've

INTRODUCTION

just ordered an oat-milk flat white) that will see me visit (on paper) some of history's most historical civilisations. And I'll be looking at the scientists, artists and writers who are part of the fabric of civilisation, as well as the first cartographers, who really put the world on the map.

Perhaps controversially, rather than put the world's historical events in alphabetical order, which seems the most logical way of doing things, I have taken the innovative approach of putting them in *chronological* order – so you can see how one thing came before another thing. It's a real eye opener. For the first time (I think) you can see the whole sweep of history *in the order it happened* – from the start of human life on the planet (the early cavemen) – to the end of it (the Cobalt Wars of 2026).

But what else makes this different from all the other complete history of the worlds? Firstly, as mentioned, it's a lot shorter, freeing up your time to concentrate on things that really matter, like emojis and self-loathing. And more obviously, what makes this unique amongst all the world's world history of the world's books is that it is illustrated, lavishly illustrated, *by its author:* me. *Philomena Cunk.* Did Sir William Churchill do his own drawings in his four-volume landmark *History of Britain*? I don't think so. And I can't be bothered to check.

The publisher (Jo was it?) did suggest that we use the services of what she called a 'professional illustrator' to do the pictures, but when I saw their work, and specifically how much it would cost, all of which would come off my advance, I said no. 'This is Philomena Cunk's History of the World,' I WhatsApped, 'the words, *and* the pictures. And I will do the audiobook as well, so you can cancel Keira Knightley, thank you very much.'*

Also of note, this is a history of the *whole* world. *For* the whole world. Because everyone, wherever they grew up, whatever their religion, has Christmas gifts to buy. And thanks to modern Western research, and violent student protests, we know now that history didn't just take place in Britain and other English-speaking countries, it took place all over the world. But let's face it, I'm writing in English, and America is the biggest market until the Chinese take over, so I'm going to be concentrating on the stuff that means something to people who can understand the language and buy things: *A History of The English-Speaking Peoples and Some Other People Who Nearly Speak English.*

Also, because pressing publishing deadlines mean that I'm writing a lot of this book from memory, and a lot of my shows have been about British people, a lot of this book is going to be British-flavoured, like crisps are. So if you're British, enjoy it, this is your history. And if you're not British, don't worry: at some point in history, you probably were.

This is also a people's history of the world, because it's written by me, a people. Maybe I didn't go to Oxbridgerton or

---

* Due to pressing deadlines, I haven't been able to draw as many pictures as I had originally planned. So some pictures are 'doubling' for various people, like when you see a play and the same actor plays a doctor and a policeman and you pretend you haven't noticed.

INTRODUCTION

Yarvard, like some of these so-called doctors of historicalese, but that's what makes this book so important: why should history be left to unknown experts, when it could be brought to life and then brought to death, by living history: me.

501 words done. Only another 49,499 to go. Let the history commencate.

IMMERSIVE HISTORY

Every so often in this book you will see a box like this – Immersive History. This contains a number of suggestions for projects, discussions, outings, exercises and other things to do that will immerse you in the historic period in question. These suggestions will help you more fully understand the history in that section and, most importantly, will go some way to furthering my word count.

Chapter One
The First Chapter

3,000,000 years BC–0 million years BC

This chapter tells the story of the first humans. It begins with men killing animals for food, and it finishes with men killing men for entertainment, which shows you how quickly civilisation developed its most important invention: leisure time – the same leisure time you're using today, to read this in between looking at your phone.

Like all history books, the early bit where there are no famous people or TV clips and it's all a bit vague is the most boring, but don't skip it because it probably has some sort of theme in it. Or a clue to who the murderer is at the end.

....

EARLY MAN

Seen here on his way to or from his cave, probably; in truth, we just don't know where he was going, it was so long ago. Most experts agree he wasn't off to the opticians, because they weren't invented then.

Cavemans

Humans like me didn't just appear, fully clothed, on the earth. Instead we had to *evolve*. And invent trousers. Trousers that fitted well but were minimal iron. Because I just don't have time to iron; we're all busy people these days, with podcasts to listen to, and puzzles to complete.

But five million years ago, when the podcast industry was in its infancy, and Wordle was still a rudimentary bony fish, some apes in Africa learned to walk upright, probably after reading how to in a book. These early humans called themselves cavemen. And cavewomen. And caveperson (they/them). They had cavechildren, formed cavefamilies, and lived in cavehouses – or 'caves' for short.

Cavemen were basically monkeys 2.0; embarrassed they'd lost all their monkey fur, cavemen hollowed out furry animals and lived inside them, walking about disguised as their own granddads.

Some cavemen were hunters, some were gatherers. The

THE FIRST CHAPTER

hunters hunted animals, and the gatherers hunted strawberries, which was easier. Hunter/gatherer tribes would move from place to place, because nobody had invented proper toilets yet and everywhere they went stank of shit.

These early humans didn't wear clothes. But even though they were naked we never see their genitals in textbooks today, although scientists believe they did have genitals and even call these first humans *Homo erectus*, as a sort of Scientists' joke.

These early people (who didn't know they were early; they thought they were on time) were interested in stones. Because this was The Stone Age.

STONEHEDGE

Stone Age man wasn't just into silly little stones. He was also into silly massive stones. They arranged giant stones into circles for no real reason, like Stonehedge, the biggest, and only, tourist attraction of its day.

Stonehedge (from the old English 'stone' meaning stone and 'hedge' meaning hedge) was used to tell the time, like a clock. But over the years the massive stone hands have dropped off and they've forgotten to wind it.

Back then, if you wanted to know the time you simply travelled to Stonehedge, and asked someone what time it was. And they would say: The Stone Age. There was no point in being more accurate than that, because by the time you got there, the time had changed and so you'd probably missed what was on at the cinema anyway. But because humans didn't invent time for another 10,000 years (and had no idea it was even taking that long), Stonehedge fell into disrepair.

CAVE ART

As well as inventing stone things, cavemen invented two other important things we have to this day: fire, which could be used to deter animals, and art, which could be used to deter people. Fire is a sort of tame gas that can be stored in sticks, and it didn't just provide warmth, it also created light, which meant cavefolk no longer had to go to sleep when the sun went off for the night. But with the iPhone still several million years away, they had to invent something to do during the long YouTube-free evenings. And so even though cavemen were just posh bears, they developed art.

This art was mainly drawing round their hands, and stick figures of animals, but it was the first step towards the great art of today, such as telling an AI computer you'd like to see a picture of *The Last Supper*, but everyone's Garfield.

The majority of cave paintings were simple stories about cows, and were made with different pigments mixed with animal fat, meaning pictures of animals were painted using animal products, which is ironic, like a lot of today's modern art is meant to be. Cavemen also believed they could contact the spirit world by doing paintings, because nobody had invented old ladies doing regional theatre

THE FIRST CHAPTER

shows where you can contact your dead gran and ask where she hid her jewellery.

But there were drawbacks to cave art. If I take a picture today, probably of my lunch, I can Instagram it round the world straight away; but cavemen paintings were stuck to rocks, so if you wanted to send it to someone, you'd have to pick up the cave and throw it, which, even when possible, is dangerous. And someone having a cave lobbed at them often doesn't have time to take in the finer points of the artwork inside. The medium is the message, whatever that means. And that's why civilisation took ages and, consequently, why this book is so long. What is it? Page 11? And we're only onto rubbish cow paintings.

When you look at cave art, it really makes you stop and pretend to think. Their pathetic daubs are, incredibly, the absolute peak of the caveman's artistic achievement: cavemen never built cathedrals or aqueducts, because they had to spend every hour of their miserable lives on the move, desperately hunting and gathering, hunting and gathering, hunting and gathering, just to put food on the table – except that they were so busy hunting and gathering that they hadn't even invented the table yet, and had to eat sitting on the floor, like schoolkids in a museum.

Life in the Stone Age must've been almost as precarious a life as working for Uber. But all that was about to change. With the invention of aggroculture.

AGGROCULTURE

Aggroculture began in a warm, moist area known as the Fertile Crescent, which sounds like a dirty term for lady parts, but isn't, because unlike your lady parts, you can see proper drawings of it in a different history book. It's located in modern-day Iraq. (The Fertile Crescent, not the different history book.)

It was in this Fertile Crescent, now called Mesopotamia, that someone first realised that instead of moving from place to place gathering bits of plant, they could grow them all in one field and have done with it. Rather than wandering about, hoping animals and crops would just walk into their mouths, they decided to cheat and just build a place where foods would be there all the time: the farm.

A farm was like a supermarket, but coming out of the ground. The first farmers domesticated animals, teaching them to give them eggs and milk and bits of themselves to turn into burgers.

Farming must have been incredibly complicated for early man when you consider that, like me, he had no idea how plants work. One of the first things the farmers invented was bread, which is mad, because you'd think that the first recipe you'd think of doing with grass would be way simpler than that. Grass and mud or something. Grass soup. Mud quiche. Grass-and-mud something else.

What even is bread? Nobody knows. But having invented bread they didn't know what to do with it, because it's only in the last twenty years that sandwiches were invented, by Pete A. Manger.

These early farmers also invented the fence. This state-of-the-art wooden forcefield meant farmers could keep animals in one place, rather than chasing them around the plains like idiots. And so humans enslaved sheep, dogs, horses and cows; the ones we couldn't eat, we sat on.

With no more need to roam, the farmers invented staying at home, one of the biggest leaps forward in all of civilisation and why we have Netflix today.

Farming meant people had time to do other stuff than look for mammoths, so they learned lots of new skills. House building. Town planning. Parkour. Civilisation had begun to begin to began.

IMMERSIVE HISTORY: CAVEMEN

1. You are a caveman. Make a list of the modern-day inventions you would miss. Carve the list onto a rock using another rock.
2. Use an iPad to do a cave painting.
3. Build a stonehedge. Use it to tell the following times:
   i) breakfast
   ii) the Bronze Age
   iii) 'Cool Britannia'
4. Invent agriculture.
5. Make up a story about two cavemen fighting each other to death over who invented fire first, really pummelling each other's heads to a fleshy pulp using sedimentary rocks.

Civlisation at Last

SUMCITY 1.0

At the start of the Bronze Age, the third best of all the ages, one of these farming communities, the Ancient Sumerians, invented making bricks. I mean, who knew you had to make bricks? It took them ages to think of bricks, considering they'd been working with stones for thousands of stupid years. Bricks had corners and didn't roll away or fall over, so were better for building houses that didn't roll away or fall over, which was useful. They used these bricks to build the first city. This city was called Ur, because when someone asked what it was called they didn't know, but that didn't matter because there was only one city anyway.

Sumerian houses were a lot like ours, except they didn't have any windows because glass hadn't been invented yet. Which meant there was nowhere to put their 'Neighbourhood Watch' stickers, which was fine because there was nowhere for burglars to climb in anyway, because they hadn't invented windows yet. Or anything worth nicking.

All these people living close together meant that Mesopotamia saw an explosion of creativity and inventioneering – it was like Silicon Valley, but ruled by Ancient Sumerians instead of weird little hipster blokes in overpriced hoodies.

THE FIRST CHAPTER

THE WHEEL

One of the Sumerians' first inventions is something that, incredibly, we still use to this day: the circle. At first they used circles to make clay spin around and evolve into pots. But pretty soon they'd made more pots than they needed, but they didn't have any easy way to move them out of their homes. Eventually out of sheer animal frustration one of them snatched the circle the clay was sitting on and tried to toss it out of sight forever. And just like that, the circle was dead, and the wheel was born.

The birth of the wheel opened up a world of business opportunities. Up until now, merchants could only transport goods as far as their arms would reach, which restricted them to selling small objects to people standing directly in front of or beside them. But now all you had to do was get a table, lob a wheel on each corner, build a small fence around it and hey bingo, you'd made a *cart*, which you could use to move your goods long distances and sell them to people in other cities, of which there were none.

MONEY MAKES THE WHEEL GO ROUND

But there was still more to invent. In fact, everything else. Until now, most trading had consisted of swapping. But it wasn't practical to swap, say, a cart full of pots for a cart full of geese, because they would get on your tits with their squawking and shitting all the way back, and now you couldn't even put the shit anywhere because you had no pots. What was needed was some sort of noiseless, shitless token that represented the value of those geese, without actually *being* geese. And that something was coin.

Because of inflation, in today's money, the value of the first coin was probably a thousandth of a hundredth of a penny, although because it's the *first* coin, it's actually worth *billions*. It's worth thinking about that, if you think about it.

Money was put into coins using a powerful magic that most people still don't understand today, which is why we only let people who've grown up with lots of money, and aren't freaked out by the magic, have most of the cash.

Money was a revolution, before it caused revolution: humans used to be worried about starving to death or being eaten by mammoths, but now they could worry about something better instead: how many of these little money circles they owned. And that's the simpler world we still live in today.

ABACUS DRABRACUS

Every upside comes with an arse side, and by inventing money the Sumerians had also invented arguments about money. People needed something to help them work out how many coins they had. But coins are round like wheels and can roll away, so the Sumerians found a way of trapping these valuable circles on a stick, where they could be counted more easily. And so they invented the abacus. At last there was a way of measuring wealth, calculating taxes (which some bastard had quietly invented already, the bastard) and keeping score at snooker. Snooker sadly wasn't invented for another 7,000 years, so it was vitally important for the Sumerians to remember who was winning in time for it to exist.

Back then, abacuses (or abaci, if you prefer, which I don't) were the most sophisticated computer the world had ever seen, because the world had never seen a computer. In a sense, the abacus was the beginning of the computer age, but it would be thousands of years before the abacus's rudimentary maze of round pills would evolve into the sophisticated Pac-Man we know today.

Before the abacus was invented, people couldn't see maths; it was invisible to the naked eye like ghosts or splinters. Suddenly, the abacus conjured maths into our dimension. And we could never go back. Even though maths makes me, and everyone, sick.

BABYLON'S FIRST WORDS

The abacus could count coins, grain, tax, sand, even how many abacuses you had. And most significantly of all it could also *store* that information. Forever. Or until someone knocked it over. But to keep the information securely in the abacus, you had to paint a picture of the abacus to remember which way up you left it. Then you had to paint a picture of the painter painting it, as a back-up.

That obvious design flaw meant they needed an even more permanent way of recording information. And that led to the next incredible invention: writing.

Writing developed as a way of keeping records of who had paid his share of crops to the temple; it was an early version of data harvesting, about actual harvesting. Incredibly, writing is still used today, to make eye-catching headlines for TikTok reels, text captions for memes, and, in a sense, even this book.

Writing probably began with people making simple marks on the ground with a stick like twits, but soon they started making marks on clay tablets. These tablets were like today's iPads but made of dried mud. You couldn't swipe on them or watch YouTube, but their battery life was amazing. In fact when archaeologists dug these tablets up, they were still working.

Writing meant that the Sumerians could make up the very first story, which was about a bloke called Gill Gamesh who has a big adventure, just like Bill and Ted. That's as much as I can tell you: even though it was published 10,000 years ago I'll get piled on if I give out any spoilers. And also I haven't read it.

But apparently bits of Gill Gamesh's story turn up in the Bible as bits of Jesus's story. Which just shows you how magic Jesus was, that he could go back in time and be in someone else's story – again, just like Bill and Ted.

THE FIRST CHAPTER

> **IMMERSIVE HISTORY: THE FIRST CIVILISATIONS**
>
> 1. Start a civilisation.
> 2. You are an Ancient Sumerian. What can you see? Why?
> 3. Reinvent the wheel. Try and patent it this time. What will you spend the royalties on?
> 4. Make an abacus from a bag of pasta shells and some twine. Ask for help from an adult when using the scissors. If you are an adult, ask yourself for help. Get something in writing in case there's an accident.
> 5. Hide in a large clay pot.

The Ancient Egypt

The invention of writing was one of those lightning strikes that never happens twice. But then it happened again – in Ancient Egypt, when the Ancient Egyptians invented it too.

Usually when you invent something again, nobody gives a shit, like in 1998 when I invented toasted sandwiches again. But the Ancient Egyptians invented writing again so well that nowadays we've heard of them and nobody gives a toss about the Sumerians. That's how well they invented it again. Instead of boring words, Egyptians wrote in pictures called hieroglyphics, which is Egyptian Latin for 'dingbats'.

So why do we remember Egyptians writing, and not the Sumerians? Why are they forgotten? Maybe it's because they hadn't invented the thing the Egyptians were really good at:

water. The thing that made Egypt grow into the top ancient empire anyone can be arsed to remember was moving water about, or 'irritation'. Irritation is when water is in the wrong place, and you get so annoyed, you move it. Once the Egyptians had dug the Suez Car Nile to shift some serious water and grow things, they invented some new things to grow: figs, dates and pomegranates, foods that, to this day, are still disgusting.

THE PYRAMIDS

When they weren't inventing fonts or flooding things, the Egyptians wore heavy eye make-up, dangly jewellery and were really into death, like Goths or Nick Cave and his Bad Seeds, but more comfortable in direct sunlight.

Until the Ancient Egyptians, dead bodies would just get kicked into some bushes like an old porn mag. But the Egyptians were different. They thought the more important you were, the more complicated your death had to be. The Egyptians preserved the corpses of their kings, or pharaohs, like pickled eggs. But they didn't keep them in jars: once they'd been mummificated ready for the next life, they needed somewhere to be stored, and as a vessel to the afterlife they needed it to be aerodynamic enough to fly up into the sky and pierce the clouds. And that's how they ended up with The Pyramid.

A pyramid was built by constructing squares of bricks on top of one another, getting more and more bored about it, so you do each level a bit smaller, with less bricks, and hope no one notices you've cut corners. The end result is

THE FIRST CHAPTER

the world's biggest monument to the art of trying to knock off early.

Today, there are still countless things we still don't know about the pyramids: how did the Ancient Egyptians get them to point exactly up at the sky? Is the design still under copyright or can anyone build one? What do pyramids run on anyway?

What we *do* know, is that the pharaohs stuffed their pyramids with all kinds of weird shit. They wanted to take all their possessions onto the other side, so they had their tombs built with no hand-luggage restrictions. Filling them up was just like packing for a holiday, except instead of putting a spare USB-C charger inside a sock they were sealing treasure and live slaves inside a crypt. And like people still do today, they way overpacked. Imagine how much worse it would have been if they'd had wheelie pyramids.

TOOTING KHAMUN

But the pyramids had a design flaw, and it wasn't just that they were uncomfortable to sit on. They were too conspicuous: huge, jewel-stuffed pyramids were a magnet for thieves. And so crafty dead pharaohs started outwitting the crooks by burying themselves *away* from the pyramids in a bit of anonymous-looking ground, just like normal dead people or pets would do. They called this place The Valet of Thee Kings.

The most famous burial site there belonged to the pharaoh Tooting Khamun. His tomb lay undisturbed for thousands of years until 1922 when British Indiana Jonesman Howard Carter cleared it out in the poshest burglary in history. The most icoconic of those treasures is Tooting Khamun's burial mask. Pharaohs had these masks made in case afterlife doormen didn't recognise them once their faces had rotted off.

Tooting Khamun was one of the biggest celebrities of his day, so it's fitting that his burial mask is a bit like the plastic surgery Hollywood stars have done: an expensive but bland impersonation of a human face crossed with a sort of cat god.

After he opened the tomb, Howard Carter and his co-thieves died one-by-one, just like everyone in *The Omen*. This has led some people to believe there's a curse on King Toot's stuff, and that if you look into his eyes, something bad will befall you. Hopefully you won't get it simply by reading about it in a book, but maybe don't travel anywhere in the next forty-eight hours, just in case.

IMMERSIVE HISTORY: THE ANCIENT EGYPTIANS

1. Try and spot a pyramid on the way to work.
2. You are an Ancient Egyptian. Do you feel seen?
3. Write out the lyrics to your favourite Radiohead song in hieroglyphics.
4. Worship the spirits of your ancestors. Or a cat.
5. Find the cheapest flight you can to Egypt and go to Egypt. I found ten days in Sharm El Sheikh, half board, for less than a thousand pounds. Can you do better?

THE FIRST CHAPTER

Ancient Greece

Meanwhile, across the Med Sea from Egypt, an even more impressive civilisation and winter-sun destination was emerging – Ancient Greeks.

The Ancient Greeks invented things that we still use today, things like triangles and sport and the name for television. The Greeks basically invented the modern school curriculum: mathematics, music, poetry, athletics, art and Greek. And they invented democracy: everyone in Greeks had a vote as long as they weren't a woman or a slave or a foreigner. It was an early example of the metropolitan liberal elite.

Democracy was developed in Greece by the Athenian statesman Solon. He was known as one of the Seven Wise Men. This is one of the few things the Ancient Greeks were wrong about – it should be *Three* Wise Men. Or Seven *Dwarves*.

The Ancient Greeks also advanced art: it was the Greeks who realised that more people would like art if they got it out of terrifying holes like caves and tombs. So they started to paint art on the walls of houses and palaces and on pots. But what they painted was filthy. It looks a bit like *Game of Thrones* made from dirt. And it was certainly dirty. You could see everything. Though most of the pots have been smashed where you can see it going in.

It wasn't all progress. The Ancient Greeks also had loads of mad ideas that seem completely nuts now, like gods being born out of each other's heads, sex with swans, and enjoying theatre.

GREEK THEATRE

The Greeks liked theatre so much they built huge open-air performance spaces, such as the Theatre of Dionysus in Athens. By today's standards it might seem pretty basic – there's no curtain, a very narrow range of flavours of interval ice cream, and the only spotlight is ninety-three million miles away. But it's got several advantages over modern theatres – it's easier to escape from, you can watch the sky when the play gets boring, it's got more ladies' toilets than the Old Vic, and best of all, it's shut.

Greek actors of the time were so famous they had to wear masks, to avoid everyone running on stage and doing selfies with them on the side of pots. Imagine the Ancient Greek tragedians performing the works of Aeschylus or Sophocles for the first time – it must have been awful.

As well as the theatre, they also built the impressive Parthenon, on top of a Cropolis hill in Athens, the centre of the Greek world. But two hundred years ago Lord Elgin took all its marbles away and put them in a British museum, in case they rolled down the hill, I suppose.

OLYMPICS

The Greeks also invented the Olympic Games. It was a bit smaller than the modern version. Mainly because they didn't consider breakdancing a proper sport, and they couldn't get sponsored by Mastercard because it didn't exist.

Athens hosted the Olympic Games every four years. There was no tendering process. Which either shows you that it was a very corrupt process, or there were no other civilisations around who wanted to bid for the games; with no TV money, they were always going to have to run at a loss.

The first Olympics Games weren't like games now: there were no controllers, no respawn points, you couldn't save halfway through if you needed to go for a poo; and the blokes who played them didn't play in their pants, they did it in no clothes at all. Men would wrestle naked with each other, all their bits out and swinging in the breeze, and say it was a sport. A bit like if Soggy Biscuit was an Olympic event now. Which maybe it is.

The nakedness was only to be expected: the first way to make money out of any new thing is to do porn on it. People would go to the stadium and download the Olympics direct to their eyes, on Private Mode, have a quick tonk, and then cheer. It was a huge success.

Sports included sexy running, sexy jumping and sexy wrestling. Women were not allowed to compete, even in the beach volleyball, making the Olympics the biggest entertainment franchise designed mainly for an audience of straight women and gay men until the invention of the Eurovision Song Contest.

There's no record of who won the first Olympics, or who came second, or even if anyone got a Lifetime Achievement

Award. On the plus side, there are no photos of naked boys, which would get it cancelled now.

Many sports we would recognise today if we watched sports – which I don't – could be seen in early 0.1 versions at the Greek Olympic Games. Before the modern pentathlon, there was the ancient pentathlon, which included stuff like minotaur jumping and a swimwear round, except it was naked.

PHILOSOPHY

Sport is mindless, so the Greeks also invented thinking, which is 100 per cent whatever the opposite of mindless is. No one had had time to think before. The Greeks even had professional thinkers, like we have today with people like Sting. *Thinking* was such a popular pastime in Greece they had a special place called the Agora, where people could gather in large groups and loudly debate ideas, like a sort of early X (formerly early Twitter) running on human meat.

This new thinking was dubbed 'philosophy', meaning they named it that. These Greek philosophers came up with bold new theories about the nature of reality and the human soul, and what's even more impressive is they were doing it all in a foreign language, Greek, which doesn't even have a fully working alphabet. We still know many of the names of these philosophers today, because they are always being copied and pasted into books like this one.

THE FIRST CHAPTER

THE FOUR GREEK PHILOSOPHERS YOU *MUST* KNOW ABOUT – YOU'LL BE AMAZED WHO'S AT NUMBER THREE

PYTHAGORAS

Pythagoras was a genius in his day, but what he looks like now will astonish you. Pythagoras invented a way of making triangles using just three lines, which is better for the environment. He believed the universe was invisibly powered by maths, like in *The Matrix*.

SOCRATES

Socrates encouraged people to incessantly question absolutely everything around them, like toddlers do. Socrates developed a system of thinking which he called The Socratic Method, because he named it after himself. The Socratic Method meant that you had to question everything: if he was here today he'd be asking me a question. But would I know the answer to it? I think I would, especially if it was multiple choice. And one of the options was a jokey answer that was obviously wrong.

Socrates never wrote anything down – so was always having to go back to the shops for things he'd forgotten. His most famous quote is 'The only thing I know is that I know nothing.' What he was saying was, he's an idiot, don't listen to him. But he wasn't an idiot, which shows you even Socrates got it wrong sometimes.

Socrates also said 'The unexamined life is not worth living.' Which basically means if you haven't taken enough Instagram photos of you doing stuff and being places, or if you haven't done enough to merit a ghost-written autobiography (like John Lennon or JFK), you're a loser. Controversial. But that was Socrates for you. And so it was no surprise that eventually the Athenian authorities made Socrates drink poison. They killed him for asking too many awkward questions, like gangsters do in black-and-white films.

PLATO

After Socrates came Plato. He invented the platonic relationship, but died before they made the film of it, *When Harry Met Sally*. (Spoiler alert: they do and then they don't and then they will and then the end.)

ARISTOTLE

Aristotle became known as the father of democracy, probably after a vote. He'd have liked that. Aristotle was a student of Plato's, but he wasn't your typical student. He believed that happiness could be found through living a balanced life, not drinking nine pints of snakebite and black in the union bar and then having a heated debate about the patriarchy.

IMMERSIVE HISTORY: THE ANCIENT GREEKS

1. Have a platonic relationship with someone.
2. Move your furniture to the edges of the living room and have a Greek-style nude wrestling match with that person. See how long you can keep the relationship platonic.
3. You are a Greek philosopher: try and have an original thought.
4. Visit the British Museum. Not to use the toilets as usual, but to look at old Greek stuff.
5. Develop a theory about triangles. Tweet it.

The Empires Trike Back

KING ALEXANDER D. GREAT

Greece became not only a hotbed for nudity and boffinism, but a huge empire, under the leadership of King Alexander D. Great. By the time he was thirty, Alexander's empire stretched all the way to India and back and forth and back and forth and forth and back.

Most people don't achieve anything like that success by the time they're thirty, so it's unrealistic to have Alexander as a role model. Basically if you're over thirty and don't rule over half the known world, relax, we're not success-shaming you. I mean, yes, *I* had my own wix.com website by thirty, but nothing else. Oh, and a two-book deal. But that was it. In terms of empires, I'd stuffed it completely.

Alexander built Greek-style buildings in his empire, like the Lighthouse of Alexandria, one of the seven wonders of the ancient world along with the Pyramints of Geezer, the Rivers of Babylon, the Statue of Dr Seuss at Kensington Olympia, The Mouse Museum at Halitosis, the Coal Lozenge of Rhodes Boyson and the Temple of Doom.

Alexander died of a fever aged just thirty-three. So maybe he had overstretched himself a bit. A warning there for you high achievers.

CHINA

Alexander's wasn't the only empire around, because empires were suddenly 'the' 'in' 'thing', like e-scooters or the Mediterranean diet. And this being a *modern* world-history book, we have to occasionally mention some places that aren't in Europe.

You may not know that, approximately around this time, China had an empire, and its first emperor, whom you've never heard of, built the Great Wall of China to keep out foreigners. But given that it's now the country's biggest tourist attraction, attracting visitors from all over the world, that counts as an epic fail. Despite its name, the wall wasn't actually built of china, because it would have shattered if someone dropped it.

The emperor eventually died and was buried with a load of clay figures – like Nick Park will be.

THE FIRST CHAPTER

ROME: EMPIRE OF VICE

But back in Europe, the most empire-y empire of them all was the Roman Empire. While the Greeks were all about fun, with their live sports and explicit bumholes, the Romans were all about power. With their advanced infrastructure, huge workforce and sophisticated amenities, the Romans were basically a sort of a posh local council in leather skirts.

The Roman Empire was so posh they all did Latin at school. And they were cutting-edge: the Romans invented concrete and aqueducts and sewers and baths and helmets with brushes on the top for pigeons to wipe their bums on.

JULIUS CAESAR

When you think of Roman emperors, you probably think of Julius Caesar. But you'd be wrong, because Caesar *wasn't* actually an emperor. An emperor rules over an empire, but in Caesar's day Rome was a republic. Meaning he was a Republican, which explains his love of war and country and western music. He was Rome's 'dictator', which back then was an official job description and not a sarcastic nickname for your boss, or your spouse.

To this day, Caesar is the only dictator to have ever had a dog food named after them, apart from Hitler Chunks which were briefly on sale in South Korea in the mid-1990s.

THE ROMAN INVASION OF BRITAIN

Under Caesar, Rome entered new territory, such as Britain, which it invaded in a sort of reverse Brexit. At this point in time Britain didn't actually have a name, so the Romans came up with one. Because they'd come here to steal our precious metals, they named the island 'Britannia', which means 'land of tin'. If they'd discovered other metals too, we could've been called 'Metallica', and would have attracted the attention of marauding Germans and Goths much earlier.

The Romans were so advanced that they soon taught the primitive locals how to wash and walk on their hind legs and to not just bite straight into cows but to use a fork. They built ruined walls, established Colchester as the new capital letter of Britain and set about introducing incredible new technologies, like mosaics, an early example of 1980s video-game pixel art which is almost still worth looking at for a few seconds today.

CAESAR'S DOWNFALL

With his sexy Egyptian girlfriend Cleopatra, Caesar was in his imperial phase. But things changed when he was named 'dictator for life' in 49 BC. Annoyed by the promotion, some tooled-up haters shanked him on the steps of the Senate, like a sort of Tupac in a big towel, and he died of knife ingestion.

Caesar's grand-nephew was known as Octavius or Augustus, depending on which bit of the Wikipedia you're looking at. Octavius/Augustus (or Augustus/Octavius) had big plans for a Roman Empire, and franchised it out around the globe, just like Starbucks. Eventually it stretched from Britain in the north, to Spain in the west, from Turkey in the east to all the other bits in the other direction. After

Octavius/Augustus came various other rulers, including Caligula, Caffé Nero, and the hi-tech iClaudius.

POMPEII

One of the reasons we still know a lot about the Romans today is because of what happened in the Roman city of Pompeii. In the seventy-ninth century AD, nearby volcano Vesuvius burped a time-stopping amount of red-hot ash on the city and its inhabitants, leaving them frozen like statues, but while doing boring things like having a shit, rather than looking noble on a horse. As they were fatally barbecued, the Pompeiians must have taken some comfort that their deaths would make a lovely day trip for people visiting the Amalfi Coast. And limoncello makers must have realised they were in for a good future. You can learn a lot from a visit to Pompeii. For example, you'll discover that an ice cream there is six fucking euros.

THE COLOSSEUM

Not all Roman cities were destroyed by Vesuvius puking its guts up. The sparkling jewel of the Roman Empire was of course Rome, chief city and jewel in the crown of the Roman Empire, known to its citizens as 'Rome'. Back then, Rome (in a Latin accent, 'Roma') was situated in Rome, as it is today. But if Rome was the jewel in the crown, there was another, even better jewel, stuck in the middle of that one: the Colosseum.

The Colosseum was an immense noisy stadium filled with spectators who had gathered to watch a group of people who might die any minute – just like a Rolling Stones concert. In its day, the Colosseum was an arena of death and misery on a par with Plymouth. And like Plymouth, once you entered, there was no way out. Except through the clearly marked exits.

The Colosseum was a sort of O2 Arena, starring murder instead of Ed Sheeran, but to very similar end effect. Crowds gathered in their manys to watch burly gladiators whittling bits off each other with swords and axes and pointy tridents. The emperor would show he was pleased or displeased using his thumbs, like the Fonz.

Gladiators wore armour, but they never wore trousers. Evidence on pots and statues show that trousers hadn't been invented by then, even though the Romans had invented a lot of deeply civilised stuff like calendars, roads, wine, saunas and being ripped to bits in public by lions. And, most importantly, Asterix. But trousers eluded them.

Gladiatorial combat was like *Bake Off* but with lions instead of cakes. Usually the lion won because, in a huge plot twist, the gladiators turned out to be the cakes. I've no idea what happened to the lions who were defeated, but they were probably turned into burgers or rugs or something.

The entertainment on offer at the Colosseum was brutal, gory, and represented Rome at its most powerful, but while confidence overflowed like the blood out of severed neck holes, little did Rome know it was about to come up against the most complex foe it had ever encountered. But that's a story for the next chapter, a chapter I'm calling 'Chapter Two'.

THE FIRST CHAPTER

IMMERSIVE HISTORY: THE ROMANS

1. Make a toga from a sheet. Ask the sheet-owner's permission.
2. Do your 'big shop' wearing only the toga. How much are the bananas? How much would they have cost in Roman times? Do a rough estimate of inflation from Roman times to now.
3. Ask ChatGPT to write a story about some Romans meeting an alien.
4. Write an essay about gender politics in Roman times.
5. Invite the neighbours over for an orgy. Keep the nibbles simple, because you don't want to keep running off to the kitchen.

THE BRICK

One of the metaphorical 'building blocks' of the Ancient World. Incredibly, still in use today, by cartoon smash-and-grabbers.

Chapter Two
Chapter Two

AD 0–1450

In this chapter I'll be talking about some old things and then some ever so slightly newer things, as I look at the Dark Ages (dark), and then the Light Ages (less dark). We're still some way off from the invention of the Nutribullet though, so if you're looking for some smoothie recipes, maybe turn to Chapter Ten. Or try my new book of healthy eating, *Deliciously Philomena*, available now at all remaining bookshops.

For non-smoothie lovers, this chapter will relate how the bright, hopeful, peaceful new religion of Christianity catapulted the world into a thousand years of ignorance, backwardness and violence.

....

JESUS PERFORMS HIS MAGIC MIRACLES

Jesus Christ remains the only religious leader to be named after a swearword, except for the nineteenth century methodistic preacher, The Reverend Simon Shit.

The Rise and Fall and Rise of Jesus Christianity

The Roman Empire was the mightiest empire the world had ever seen. But it was about to be smashed to bits by a man better known for knocking up spice racks: the radicalised carpenter Jesus Christ.

Jesus was a man-stroke-god who would have a huge impact on philosophy, religion, science, architecture, hate and art for the next 2,000 years. It's amazing to think that without Jesus and Christianity, there'd be no Notre Dame, no Sir Paul's Cathedral and no 'I like the pope, the pope smokes dope' T-shirts.

THE RISE OF JESUS

To follow the rise of Jesus, we need to go back in time to the birth of Christ, four years before the birth of Christ, in 4 BC, in the Roman-controlled Holly Lands.

Jesus Christ was named after the first thing his father, Joseph, said when his wife said she was up the spout by a ghost. Jesus became a carpenter, but foreseeing the eventual rise of flat-pack furniture, and realising he had transferrable skills, Jesus switched careers to become the very first motivational lifestyle guru, going from place to place doing miraclising to raise his profile and get likes.

THE FALL OF JESUS

Christ only really 'went viral' after his death, a bit like a Russian teenager who's fallen off a skyscraper on TikTok.

His execution was inevitable: it was little wonder this influential handyman-turned-magician scared the Roman authorities. They considered Jesus so dangerous they had him crucified. Being nailed to a wooden cross was an especially cruel punishment considering he was a carpenter, as he'd have hated the substandard craftsmanship involved. Presumably if he'd been a butcher they'd have slowly minced him to death, which would've been worse, although chances are that thought provided little comfort in his final moments on the cross, examining the clumsily constructed dovetail joints of the cross beam at close quarters.

THE RISE OF JESUS PART II

Once he was dead, Christ's body was taken down from the cross, which must've been quite a job given all the nails they'd used to keep him up there. I imagine they used the bendy end of the hammer. Then he was wrapped in a Turinese shroud and put in a cave for safekeeping.

But incredibly, like a proper showman, Jesus had saved his greatest miracle for after he died, when he magicked himself alive again. Even David Blaine would say that was a strong finale, but Christ was only just getting going.

Jesus had preached for just three years, and only had twelve followers while he'd been alive. That's because back then, people had to take likes and retweets from town to town by hand. So for the time being, 'word of mouth' remained the most popular means of getting your message out there and building brand awareness amongst target demographics.

THE GODSPELS

A man called Saul spread the world of Jesus across Europe. We know him today not as Saul but as Saint Paul, so either he did a Jedward/Brangelina thing with Saint and Paul, or he didn't know his own name in the first place, which makes you wonder what else he got wrong.

We only know what Jesus said through the gospels that were written down by John, Luke, Paul and Ringo, the fab four, but soon the whole world was picking up on the moptop quartet's simple, hopeful messages, such as 'Help!', 'We Can Work It Out' and the one about being an egg. Biblemania was born.

ROMANS AND PERSECUTION OF CHRISTIANS

But in Rome, the Emperor Nero blamed Christians for everything, from burning down the city to an outbreak of obesity in lions. In Rome, Christians were persecuted, which is Latin for 'shat on'. As a result, Christians in Rome were forced to meet in secret in the catacombs underneath Rome, where they could spread the word of God and have jumble sales in peace.

Romans started throwing Christians into the Colosseum with lions, to see who would eat who first. Maybe the Christians hoped they could convert the big cats from lionism to Christianity in the few seconds their vocal cords were intact. But it wasn't to be. For one thing, the lions had their own Jesus, called Simba. And for another, they were more interested in eating Christians than listening to their fucking parables. It didn't help that the Christians made it easy for the lions by constantly turning the other cheek, like a sort of self-rotating doner kebab.

It soon became clear Christians and lions weren't capable of sharing the Colosseum in peace – and a two-state solution was nowhere to be found. It was the beginning of the war between Christians and lions that continues to this day. They still can't so much as share a tent together without it all kicking off.

Incredibly, the war between Christians and Romans was short-lived by comparison. In fact within a few hundred years, the Romans were well into Jesus themselves after

Roman Emperor Constantine got the Christ virus and breathed it on anyone in Rome who wasn't wearing a mask – which was everyone.

THE FALL OF ROME

Despite Rome's born-again piousness, disaster was waiting round the corner. Rome had changed to a religion of peace and love just in time to have its arse handed to it in a bag by some people who mainly believed in hammers and smashing.

Over the preceding centuries, Rome had invaded everywhere, but suddenly everywhere decided to pop round and return the favour: gangs of Vandals and Goths ruined the city, just like they would do centuries later in Wolverhampton. The Vandals wanted to smash Rome up and paint cocks all over it. And unfortunately for the Romans, thanks to their own ground-breaking transportation network, all roads led to Rome, which made it very easy for the Vandals to get there. They didn't even have to use Citymapper.

It was anarchy. Rome hadn't seen such debauchery and violence since a few days earlier; but this wasn't in the Colosseum, it was in the streets, interactive and in your face, like modern theatre, and just as unbearable.

With Romans versus everyone else, the fall of Rome was like the First World War.*

---

* So that makes World War I into World War II. And that makes World War II into World War III. So that means I don't have to worry about World War III any more as it's already happened. Thank God that's off the table.

CHAPTER TWO

Rome was sacked. It didn't even get to take its stuff out in a cardboard box and walk sadly to the lifts. The city was on fire, and not in the good sexy 'peak you' sort of way, but in the actually-on-fire-burning way. Soon the fire spread, and burning Rome down turned out to be all it took to collapse the whole Roman Empire.

Rome had come out publicly as a Christian and got bashed in by the bigger, rougher kids. It's a story as old as time. Well, it happened to Fiona Belson at my school, and we all got shit for it, so it's sort of the same.

IMMERSIVE HISTORY: EARLY CHRISTIANS

1. You are a Christian in the Colosseum: how close do you let the lion get before reappraising your relationship with Jesus?
2. Write your own Lord's Prayer. What would you ask for every day? Be specific, so 'Hula Hoops', not just 'crisps'.
3. Write a fifth gospel that would speak to today's self-obsessed youth.
4. Do a miracle.
5. Paint a picture entitled 'Jesus v. Harry Potter'. Do not infringe any copyright material.

The Dark Ages Cometh

Whatever the reason for Rome's demise and Fiona Belson's move to another school, one thing was clear: the end of Rome meant it was time for the Dark Ages.

We don't know what happened in the Dark Ages, because it was so dark. No one could see what was going on, and even if they glimpsed something by candlelight, they couldn't find their quill to write it down. But it's doubtful that, before the advent of global streaming services and Instagram, anything really noteworthy was happening anyway.

WHAT IS A THE DARK AGES?

A Dark Ages is what we call the time when the world stopped being civilised. Before the Dark Ages, there was Roman civilisation (lots of killing and disease and unfairness and mad stuff) and after it, there was the Renaissance (lots of killing and disease and unfairness and mad stuff, but really good paintings of it).

The main way to tell that an age is a Dark Age is if the paintings of it are a bit flat and wonky and the eyes don't line up, like the characters are painted on the side of a waltzer. If the castles in the background of a painting are actually in the background, rather than balancing on Jesus's head, and the people have their eyes in a straight line, it's probably not a The Dark Age, it's just an age.

Some historians don't like the term 'Dark Ages' because

they think it's insulting; apparently plenty of good science and ideas were around in the Dark Ages, but you won't have heard of them. That makes it quite a hipster sort of time, which probably explains the ludicrous beards and all the stupid shoes.

Around the twelfth century, Europe stopped stumbling about in the dark, found the light and switched it back on, joining the rest of the planet in the Non-Dark Ages, but only after it had (in historical terms) tripped over the cat, stubbed its toe, and produced some of the wonkiest-eyed art in history.

THE DARK AGES AROUND THE WORLD

The Dark Ages might've been the end of civilisation as we know it, but luckily Europe wasn't the only country having a history back then. We now know that other countries, like South America and the Far East, have history too.

Uncovering the secret histories of these faraway places was thought impossible for thousands of years, until modern research methods, like asking people who lived there and writing it down, were invented by European history boffins.

Historians now insist that while everyone in Europe was blundering about forgetting the Latin for everything, stepping on the cat, and having their eyes on a wonk, life in not-Europe was tickety-boo, with people happily strolling about in bright sunshine, inventing the printing press, noodles and long division.

ANCIENT CHINA

People in China would have had no idea they were even in a Dark Age. The message just hadn't got through; even if they had been able to invent a sort of eighth-century Chinese Zoom video conferencing system, nobody in Europe knew how to build another one to receive the call and see all the faraway Chinese activity, because they were too busy sitting in the dark, dying of a plague and bumping into stuff.

Just like today, China was working much, much harder than it needed to, and Europeans were sat around on our arses waiting for them to get on with it. China invented absolutely everything, but then refused to show it to anyone, like when your mate says they've got an amazing new boyfriend but he goes to a different school so you'll never meet him. So we have to take their word for it, but apparently the Chinese invented clockwork machines, air conditioning, gunpowder and loom bands.

Not everything the Chinese invented worked. They tried to build a silk road to the west, but of course, that was doomed to failure: silk is just too delicate for any kind of permanent transport link.

The Chinese were very discreet about their inventioning. Chinese writing is made of little drawings of houses and stick men, which means that even if Europeans had got hold of the plans for a Chinese clockwork dog or a gunpowder, we would have thought it was just a cartoon, like 'Garfield'. Their secrets were safe.

Paper

Chinese art was developing too, mainly in China, and it is notable for one important development: the invention of paper. This was probably the biggest revolution ever to happen in China.

Still to this day, no one knows how paper is made. But it instantly made all previous inventions seem like something you wouldn't wipe your arse with. Paper was a revolution for pictures. Now art could be portable – it didn't have to be on a wall or in a tomb. And importantly, that meant portable pornography. Now you could get aroused in the privacy of your own hut, rather than in the town square with all the other perverts.

Printing

What's more, by achieving 'paper', the Chinese had also unlocked the ability to invent printing. Early printing worked by carving letters – or in the case of Chinese, random lines – onto wooden blocks, which could then be arranged into words, or whatever the Chinese equivalent of words is. These words were then dipped in ink and pressed onto paper – where they could be looked at by literally anyone who could be arsed. The early printing method was a laborious process, almost as difficult and boring as reading itself.

PROPHET MUHAMMAD AND ISLAMIC EXPANSION

While the Chinese were busy inventing paper, at the same time but hundreds of years later, in Arabia, a prophet called Muhammad was coming up with another world-changing invention: Islam, which I'm not going into detail about here. There just isn't room.[*]

---

[*] For more information on this subject see my *Illustrated History of Islam*.

CHAPTER TWO

England in the Dark Ages

As with the rest of Europe, with the Romans gone, Britain was left on its own. It had taken back control from the unelected bureaucrats of Europe and was free at last to explore its own proud destiny. We don't know a huge amount about what actually happened in England in the Dark Ages because the Romans had taken the last pens with them, and that's probably why it became a time of myth and great real-life heroes, like King Arthur, the King Of The Arthurs.

KING ARTHUR

If you think knife crime is bad now, you should have been around in Arthur's time. According to English legend, it is said that King Arthur became king after pulling a sword from a stone, when probably who you really want as a king is the man that *put* the sword in the stone. He would have been built like a brick shithouse.

King Arthur lived in a castle called Camelot, where he invented a Round Table for his knights; I'm surprised that King Arthur had a round table, when he could have saved so much space with an extending table with retractable wings, like my mum has done since Dad moved out. Looking at the names on the Round Table now, it's amazing how humble the knights were, as not one of them insisted on OBE after their names.

It's incredible to think of the knights who would be

sitting at the Round Table today – Sir Paul McCartney, Sir Cliff Richard, Sir Andrew Lloyd Webber, Sir Elton John. Not men you would send to kill a dragon, but any of them could put on a very successful jukebox musical.

THE NORMAN CONQUEST

A few hundred years after mythical Arthur's mythical death, a whole new generation of wannabe overlords started arguing over who should be in charge of England. The contenders were William of Normandy, who thought he should be king, and Harold Godwinson of England, who very much thought William shouldn't, what with William of Normandy coming from faraway Normandy, and Harold already actually being King Harold of England.

Some historians believe that in 1064 Harold had been shipwrecked in Normandy, and William came to his aid. In exchange for his help, William made Harold swear an oath that he'd help William become king of England. It was sort of like one of those timeshare sales events where you sign a piece of paper just to make it all go away, and hope no one will remember about it later.

But William did remember and it all kicked off. Halley's Comet appeared in the sky when Harold was coronated. The comet was considered an omen. But not a good omen, like *The Omen*. But a bad omen, like the remake of *The Omen*.

William decided to settle the matter with a Battle of Hastings.

CHAPTER TWO

1066: A BATTLE OF HASTINGS

1066 – it's not just my PIN number, it's the most important year in British history. Which is *why* it's my PIN number.*

1066 was a conflict that was to change the course of English history, but even though it was such an important event, there're no films about it, possibly because no Americans were involved, or because the *Carry On* team had all died before they got round to it.

Harold and William's armies met at Hastings and, incredibly, we've got an accurate visual record of the whole battle because of the Bayeux Tapestry – a panoramic photograph of the battle made of wool. It was downloaded line by line, like dial-up internet pornography about arrows.

The battle was decisive: William stuck an arrow in Harold's eye, radically changing his prescription and meaning he'd need new glasses. Before he could even book an eye test, Harold died, William took control, and Britain was suddenly part of Europe. It was a disaster from which proud Britons would only recover by never overthrowing the conquering king and letting his descendants still be in charge today.

---

* Impossible to forget, and yet totally secret and personal to everyone in Britain.

CASTLES

Castles are very big houses with tops that look a bit like proper pies with eggs in.

Castles was always hives of activity, even before they were tourist attractions or locations for filming re-enactments, because, as well as being strategic strongholds, castles had another purpose: they also had a gift shop, where peasants could buy smelly rubbers and chocolates with a portcullis on the box.

CHAUCER

After a long day of kinging or minstrelling or jestering or princessing, the people who lived in castles could relax with the latest blockbuster comedy by Chaucer. Geoff 'Ray' Chaucer's greatest work was *The Canterbury Tales*, a sort of an anthology box set, like *The Twilight Zone* or *The World at War*. Chaucer's stories were collected in a new format that would prove very popular until the start of the twenty-first century – the book.

Chaucer found favour in royal circles, and King Edward the Three granted him a reward of a gallon of wine a day for the rest of his life, so it's surprising that Chaucer wrote anything at all. That's two wine boxes *a day*. For life. Think about it. What did Chaucer say when his doctor asked him how many units he drank a week? Just a couple of gallons?

When he died (well, a bit after, not the exact moment), Chaucer was the first poet to be buried in Poets' Corner at Westminster Abbey. Before him, it was just called 'the corner'. And it wasn't that sought after as a burial spot.

KING JOHN AND MAGDA CARTER

King John liked fighting wars abroad but, like a smoker, needed more money to fund his filthy habit. He demanded more taxes from the nobility, but the Baron Knights rebelled and forced him into negotiations.

They said the King shouldn't be in charge, because not all kings make good decisions. Just look at King Kong. Or King Rollo. Or Burger King.

The Baron Knights made him sign a deal with a woman called Magda Carter, a set of laws that limited the power of the King and gave humans rights, something that the powers that be are still trying to stop to this day.

King John signed Magda's contract even though he didn't want to. And in those days there was no 'fourteen-day cooling-off period'. That was enshrined in the later Consumer Rights Act 2015.

The Magda Carta was considered ahead of its time, because one of its clauses deals with the mis-selling of PPI.

It was written on sheepskin with a feather quill, and sealed with beeswax, which means that, like the five-pound note and Haribo Starmix, the Magda Carta is not vegan. It's incredible to think that if this important document caught fire, British civilisation would go up in smoke with it. It would immediately be a lawless hellhole and we'd be having sex in the street and shitting in bins.

SCOTLAND'S SAVIOUR: WILLIAM WALLACE

Meanwhile, fortuitously, the Middle Ages was also happening in Scotland at the same time as in England. In 1296, Scotland was reluctantly under the rule of English King Edward Fox. But Scotsman William Wallace wanted out; without the SNP to vote for, he gathered an army and defeated the English at Stirling Bridge, but was then captured by the English. He was taken to London where he was found guilty of treason and simultaneously hung, drowned and quilted.

There was a big audience for his execution; because there was no entertainment in those days, people didn't even really have a good idea what would be entertaining. They thought that watching a man have his bowels chopped out might be a bit of a grin. These days, when the masses want to see someone publicly maimed, they just look at social media.

Wallace's head was placed on London Bridge, and his limbs were sent to Scotland. But there was no one in when they tried to deliver them, so they left a 'while you were out' card.

THE CRUSADES

In 1095, Christian Europe decided that the Muslims needed help; specifically, they needed Jesus's love stabbed into them.

CHAPTER TWO

The kings of Europe (who sound like the kind of disappointing band who go on at a festival at about 11 a.m. when everyone's still in their tents) were all fighting and rowing with each other. So the Pope decided to pull a huge 'look over there' stunt and did a sermon telling Christians from all over the continent to go on a sort of violent cruise, called a crusade – from 'cruise-', meaning cruise, and '-ade', meaning 'fizzy'. He said Christians should drive the Muslim Turks out of Palestine and retake Jerusalem. And so began a feud as old as Lamar v. Drake, possibly even older: Christians v. Muslims.

Soon armies from Europe set off for a good international kicking. It was a time of men on horses in metal hats. The first crusading armies were under the leadership of Peter the Hermit who, instead of living in a hut and tying his trousers up with string like most hermits, decided to take the helm of an international fighting force.

It took them three years to reach the Holy Land, because you're not meant to rush a cruise, and in the year £10.99 the Christians captured Jerusalem. But then the Muslims, under their leader Saladin (no relation to Aladdin), started a crusade of their own, and they retook Jerusalem.

By now, everyone was really into the crusades. They were more popular than *Game of Thrones*. So they kept doing them – there were four in total. There were less tits and dragons than *Game of Thrones* admittedly, but for a primitive attempt at long-running entertainment, the crusades had plenty of exciting violence and powerplay, and you really never knew who'd die next, which made for some great cliffhangers. Three and a half stars.

> **IMMERSIVE HISTORY: THE EARLY MIDDLE AGES**
>
> 1. You are a peasant in the Dark Ages. What are you doing reading this book? Books haven't been invented yet.
> 2. Design and build an astrolabe, without googling what an astrolabe is.
> 3. Sing a madrigal with a loved one.
> 4. Go on a crusade against the Turks.
> 5. Write a modern re-telling of a *Canterbury Tale* and see if anyone at all is interested in it. You can get a grant from the Arts Council.

The Mongol Empire

The crusades were a box-set war fought in a far-off land over religion, but soon one man would start a real fight for the survival of civilisations as we know it. Which wasn't much back then.

In the twelfth century, Mongol big cheese Genghis Khan was the most feared man on earth, famed for his brutality and power. It was like if Freddy Krueger was President: people everywhere were shitting it. Khan and his Mongol bastards brutally mowed down everyone in their path across much of Europe and Asia (the landmass collectively known as Erasure) as they conquered the shit out of everything they laid eyes on.

Millions and thousands of people were mercilessly slaughtered to death. Many of them got their heads chopped off. Others had their legs hacked off first, then an arm or something, and then maybe their face, which was probably still screaming as it flew across the hut or wherever they lived. Then the invaders might've taken the carcasses and hacked them all up and boiled them into soup and carved all the discarded pelvis bones into big ladles to drink it with, and then sat around the fireplace slurping their deathly soup and laughing and blowing off. I mean it was *seriously* out of order.

Genghis Khan killed so many people that farmland returned to woodland, and global temperatures went down. Let's hope this doesn't give today's green movement any ideas. It's bad enough having to recycle as it is.

The Plague

In the fourteenth century, Europe faced a different invasion from the east. It wasn't a person or any army or a meme, it was a plague: the Black Death, carried by fleas, which were carried by rats, which were carried by sailors in their wooden legs. The filthy, cramped living conditions of the age meant the plague cut through the population like a mad hairdresser. It transformed Europe, from a place full of normal people to a place full of dead people.

These days, when we have plagues, we call them 'pandemics' and there's less rats but loads more rules. And we brand them better. 'Black Death' is a proper shitter of a name; 'COVID-19' just sounds like a disappointing computer from years ago.

Joan of Arc

Despite being called Joan, which is a very British-sounding name, Joan of Arc wasn't a woman your mum knows from Pilates. She wasn't even from Arc, actually. She was from France, which was another country that was trying to live its best life in its Middle Ages.

Joan of Arc was as religious as a person can get without turning into a stained-glass window. When she was just thirteen she claimed to have been visited by three saints – Michael, Catherine and Margaret. Again – very British names. I'm just saying: it's odd isn't it?

At the time of Joan's Arc, the English occupied most of northern France, but the saints told Joan to drive them out and Make France Great Again.

So she sought out the King of France, who was called Charles – which is as British a name as it gets. This is getting stupid. Anyway, she asked him to make her the head of his army and, even though she was a mentally unstable teenager with zero military experience, he said yes, which perhaps gives some insight into the kind of decision-making that had led to Charlie losing half of France in the first place.

Joan snuck into enemy territory disguised as a man, in a brave act of non-binary soldiering, and incredibly, led the French troops to victory before being captured by the English who put her on trial for heresy and cross-dressing, in an early example of right-wing anti-woke transphobia.

She was burned at the stake, which wasn't just cruel, but environmentally unfriendly to boot. And this being France, she probably wasn't even cooked through properly and was still *very* rare inside when she died. Bleu.

In her short life, Saint Joan had risen from humble servant girl to delusional lunatic to martyred saint, burnt at the stake for her beliefs. A real Cinderella story. Well, the 'Cinders' bit at any rate.

Dan Tay and *The Divine Comedy*

Chaucer wasn't the only bookist demonstrating a mastering of word-using in the Dark Ages. Written in 1308, *The Divine Comedy* by Dan Tay was the blockbuster book of the era; it was the *Da Vinci Code* of Da Vinci times. *The Divine Comedy* came to define the Medieval worldthing.

It tells of the author's travels to the afterlife, a bit like the film *Ghost*. It's what's called an epic poem, which means it's far too long, and it's set in both heaven and hell, so it sounds like a classic next-door-neighbours-who-don't-get-on sitcom. Although, for a comedy, it's actually quite serious and full of suffering instead of jokes. Which must mean it's a modern comedy.

The Divine Comedy was a big hit, mainly because it was a relief to have something other than the Bible to read. Yet because there was no printing press, there was no way for *The Divine Comedy* to be distributed, so nobody could see it, a bit like when something's only on Paramount Plus. But all that was about to change . . .

It's time for Chapter Three of this book. Which you are only holding in your hands because of a man called Gutenberg's invention. And the Chinese seven hundred years before him.

A CASTLE

You can still see castles to this day, by looking at pictures of castles, like this one.

Chapter Three
The Third Chapter

AD 1450–1620

In this chapter in this book of all the things that ever happened in order, or 'history' of the earth, we will see how the Renaissance turned Europe from a load of mud and parsnips into a posh destination resort full of paintings and cherubs. I'll be looking at how the ages went from dark to slightly less dark. It's a chapter about how the world got woke – not to sexual harassment and climate change – but to the wisdom of the Ancient Geeks. It was time for the Renaissance.

....

COLUMBUS' VOYAGE

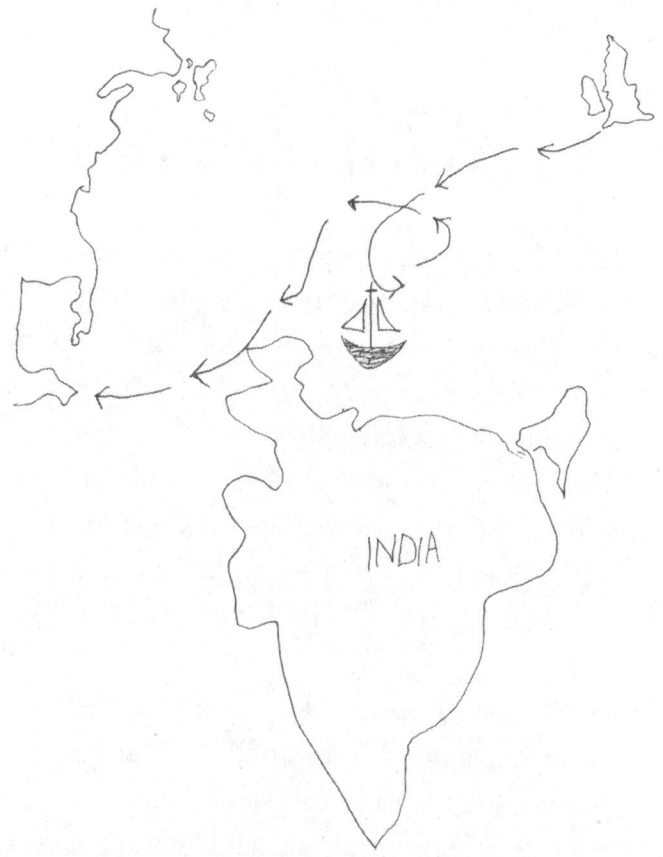

If Columbus was correct, and you could get to India by heading West, then it would have re-written the map of the world. As it is, it stayed the same, and India remains where it has always been, wherever that is.

Renaissance — *as in the dictionary* ↓

The Birth of the Renaissance

What is the Renaissansse? Apart from impossible to spell correctly the first time every time you write it, even if, like me, you're having to write it every other word for a chapter about it. It's got too many 'n's in it and looks wrong whether you put in four, or nine.

Perhaps more importantly, what started the Renayssancce? To find out, we have to go back in time. Further back than the Remaisssonce I've only just mentioned. Back to a time I've already done in an earlier chapter. Ancient Greece. Again.

As you'd know if you'd been paying attention during the first chapter, and didn't drift off listening to the audiobook, Ancient Greece was smart-alec Ground Zero, where megaboffins like Aristotle, Plato and the other ones all jostled for brain supremacy. If you've *already* forgotten that then go and read that chapter again. Then come back here.

Now.

It's on page 23.

Done it?

Okay, then we can carry on.

To continue: after the Greek supernerds died and turned into statues of the bits down to their shoulders, their theories lived on outside their dead minds, because they'd been written down. But still, the idea didn't gain much worldwide airplay, because the one thing no one was doing back in the Middle Ages was reading a book; not because nobody in their right mind reads a book, but because nobody had invented the printing press, so there was only one book, and it belonged to the king. But then something amazing happened: a man called Gutenberg invented the printing press. (Again.)

THE PRINTING PRESS

The printing press was very much the internet of its day.

Until the invention of the printing press, books had to be painstakingly copied by hand by monks, who just churned out the Bible again and again, rather than trying something different like a play by Plato or even the latest Harlan Coben. As a result, people were trapped in an echo chamber of ancient Christian texts – any writing that wasn't just 'the Bible' with big colourful capital letters in it was unavailable, even online. It was worse than keeping making *Spider-Man* over and over again, because at least he spins webs. To be fair, Jesus had hands that could shoot out loaves and fishes, and he could fly out of a cave, but the story was getting old.

So it was no surprise that the first thing to be pressed out on Gutenberg's printer, once he'd got the wi-fi set up and the paper in the slot, was the Bible. Because sometimes you have to know where the money is.

To stop the printing press just becoming a religious photocopier, Gutenberg had a go at printing other things, like a psalter, which is a book containing the psalms, so in other words, a sort of mini-Bible. This disappointing follow-up might be the first instance of Difficult Second Album Syndrome.

But once people realised there could be things other than the Bible, they saw the possibilities of the printer: you could take any crazy theory you could think of, print it in thousands of leaflets, and run around shoving those into people's hands. Like mad people still do today.

Soon leaflets turned into pamphlets, which evolved into books. 'Books' were a sort of PDF file you could touch. Incredibly, a book is actually what you are holding right now. Unless you're listening to the audiobook, in which case you have something else in your hands. You'll have to take a look yourself and see what it is. It's probably a steering wheel if you're driving. Or a coffee if you've just bought a coffee. Like I have.

Gutenberg's press kick-startered the book industry. Without Gutenberg we'd have nothing to read on the train, or the toilet. Apart from our phones.

WHAT ARE BOOKS?

Books are rectangular, like a phone, except there's only one thing on the 'screen' at a time. Instead of swiping, you have to 'turn' a 'page'. Try it now – but make sure you make a note of this page so you can return to it. You can use the notes app on your phone to do this.

What you do is, you very gently lift the 'corner', and then you sort of carry it over to the other side, and release. And then you have to do that hundreds more times.

And that's books.

COPYRIGHT-FREE CONTENT

Now ideas and science and shit could all be written in a book and everyone could read it, as long as they were the 0.1 per cent of the population that could read and had the time to do so. Soon, the printed word would start to spread not just the word of God, but the word of scientists, philosophers and other scientists who didn't agree with the first lot of scientists.

Dark Age man devoured books with their eyes, and soon this cutting-edge platform was crying out for fresh content, like Amazon Prime is today. So people started digging through forgotten old material to see if it could be remastered in 'book' format. That's how the clever ideas of Ancient Greece suddenly came back in fashion, centuries after the Ancient Greeks themselves had died. This newfound fame sadly came too late for the Greek superbrains: Isosceles, for example, never got to enjoy any of the royalties from his triangles and died buried in a humble toga in a simple triangular grave.

But still, the effect of all this Greek knowledge suddenly becoming available for a new generation was transformative – a reboot in disguise. It was time for ... the Renaisianciance.

THE RENAISSANCE (CHECK SPELLING)

As far as medieval folk were concerned, everyday existence had always been as tough and joyless as my Uncle Martin, who's an absolute cunt. He's never going to read this, so I'm not worried about him seeing it.

Medieval people believed all this grim backbreaking toil was the way things were supposed to be. The only pleasant experiences they had were dying of buboes or watching other people having a worse time than they were, hanging from the gallows.

So for them to read about how the Ancient Greeks and Romans were into art and thinking was like taking a mind-expanding drug that would permanently transform the way they saw themselves. Just like when my mate Paul ate five ketamine brownies and became convinced he could communicate telepathically with any animal he saw on television. Although whereas Paul ended up sectioned for his own safety, our Renaissance ancestors decided to change the world.

It was a cultural 'rebirth', but to make it sound extra arty, they used the French word for 'rebirth' – Renaissance. It refers to a rebirth of learning in Europe, a thing that Renaissance people only found out was happening now they were able to learn French. (Before the Renaissance, even the French didn't understand what they were saying, and communicated mainly by shrugging and smoking. They still do.)

For hundreds of years, in the Dark Ages, all anyone had cared about was horse-riding, arrows and court jesters. Life was simple. But suddenly everyone was really clever and liked books. For the first time in centuries, they didn't just look up the rude bits or draw dicks on the pictures. Even the biggest swots didn't get a single wedgie or a bogwash. Learning was cool. It was like *Sesame Street,* but in coloured tights and ruffs. There was such excitement that nobody stepped in, and soon, sadly, there was Shakespeare, and maths and science, and school was ruined forever.

HUMANISM

A new type of thinking was invented: Humanism, the belief that art, music and science are as essential to human existence as going to the toilet, or having a face. Painters and thinkers began to explore new ideas based on ancient learning – basically doing cover versions without the permission of the original artists, which, given the gap of a thousand years or more, would have been hard to obtain in any case, even if both parties had been in broad overall agreement of the terms.

THE ART SCENE

One of the most amazing things that happened in the Renaissance is that everyone remembered how to draw properly. The Greeks and the Romans and their friends were really good at drawing. But for the whole of the Dark Ages, everyone was dogshit at it. A simple game of Pictionary could last decades.

In the Dark Ages, everything was side on, like *Super Mario*. But the Renaissance turned that into *Super Mario 64*. One day, everyone remembered how many fingers were on a hand, and how to do horses. It was like in a film where someone gets bonked on the head and turns Spanish for a bit, and then gets another bonk on the head and turns back. Although I have never seen a film where that happens.

NEW PERSPECTIVES ON NEW PERSPECTIVES

European art had been absolutely bloody awful for ages. And this was the professional stuff. Suddenly, the Renaissance artists were miles better. And this was centuries before Bob Ross.

One of the most important things that the Renaissance reinvented was perspective. Before perspective, there was no such thing as stairs, and they were just floorboards. So the only way to go upstairs was to do that *Star Trek* thing where you disappear and turn up somewhere completely different. It's called 'teleportation', and it was very much the witness protection programme of its time.

THE THIRD CHAPTER

BOTTICELLI

One notable artist of the time was Botticelli. Despite being one of the few Renaissance artists not to have a secret identity as a Teenage Mutant Ninja Turtle, he did paint the original hero in a half shell – Venus, the Roman Goddess of Love. *The Birth of Venus* is believed to depict the world's first celebrity wardrobe malfunction. Venus is naked, though she's managed to cover up most of the interesting bits of herself with an arm and some hair.

MICHAELANGELOSS DAVID

But perhaps the most stunningly accurate human figure to come out of the Renaissance is a statue of an extremely naked man called Michaelangeloss David. Some people think his penis looks small, but when you bear in mind he's five metres tall, his dick's actually about the size of a small dog, and it's not even at action stations yet.

VINCI D. A.

Michaelangeloss was pretty good at art. But he had a rival, the Super Nintendo to his Sega Megadrive: Leonardo Da Vinci.

Leonardo Da Vinci was what we call a 'Renaissance man' because he was a man. And he lived in the Renaissance. But he wasn't just a man – he was a genius who filled thousands of notebooks with amazing ideas. Like we all have.

To this day he's the only person in history to have finished a notebook, (and not just signed his name eighteen times on the first page then decided to move on to a new one).

But it's for his paintings we know him today. Da Vinci's most famous is the *Moaner Lisa*. Even today people queue for hours to see it, even though there's no need to because you can see it outside, on your phone. Or on a tea towel or fridge magnet. Or basically anywhere. It's probably in your hair somewhere.

The *Moaner Lisa* is a great example of perspective, because to see her you have to look over the heads of a crowd of tourists to pick out this tiny painting a long way off. It's weird that she's called a moaner, because she doesn't look that pissed off. Although she might be fed up because she hasn't got any legs. Seems a bit unfair, doesn't it? Lisa the Moaner doesn't even get her legs painted, but Michaelangeloss David gets his tinkle modelled. Bit sexist, if you ask me.

Also, she doesn't look like a Lisa. She looks more like a Barbara or a Glenys. So maybe she was using a stage name.

If she'd known how famous she'd become, she might have made a bit more effort and pulled one of those Caitlin Moran faces – you know, head on one side, wide eyes, big gasp. Maybe even a streak through her hair. Something with a bit of rizz. As it is, she looks more like Bored Lisa than Moaner Lisa. The sort of person who'd tell you to turn your phone off in a library.

> **IMMERSIVE HISTORY: THE RENAISSANCE**
>
> 1. Paint an Sistine Chapel. Ask the Sistine Chapel's owner's permission first.
> 2. Use GarageBand (or similar) to record a rap/dance track about man's place in the universe.
> 3. Bake a cake that celebrates the best of Renaissance thinking.
> 4. Host a murder mystery dinner loosely themed on the invention of the printing press.
> 5. Imagine a conversation between Da Vinci and the Moaner Lisa as he painted her. It was probably mainly him because she'd have to keep her lips still until the paint dried.

Christopher Columbus Discovers America

Even during the intellectually flowering Renaissance, people were still incredibly ignorant about the planet. Like they are today. Large areas of the world were completely unknown to the people of medieval Europe. This was an age of maps with all the countries the wrong shape and sea dragons in the corners. They knew about China, India and Africa, even if they thought they were covered in mermaids and Loch Ness Monsters, but no one had any idea that America even existed. Fuckwits.

Traders from Europe wanted to find a quicker route to India but were scared of sailing too far because back then they thought the world was flat, like some of us are starting to realise it is today.

But one man dared to dream it wasn't flat: Saint Christopher Columbus. He set sail in the wrong direction to find India's back door. Everyone thought Columbus was nuts and that he and all the sailors in his three ships would fall off the side of the world into some sort of overflow cistern underneath the earth with bits of hair and blobs of old soap like you get at the bottom of a shower.

But everyone was wrong. Including Columbus. He didn't find the Orient Express route, but discovered a land that was to have a massive impact on the history of the world from that point onwards: he'd discovered The Bahamas. And suddenly the world had a brand-new winter-sun holiday destination and money-laundering hub.

Columbo's voyage was a failure in that he totally failed to find India. But it was also a success because his ship eventually bonked into a faraway land no one in Europe had even realised was there: America. Columbus was the first person to find America, apart from the millions of people who were living there already. He called the place he discovered the Nude World, because the natives there were barely dressed. Columbus returned home from America with wonders from the continent, and a bag of Hershey's Kisses for the office.

THE AMERICAS

After Columbus discovered America, loads of other people fancied discovering it too. Soon it had become a prime shopping destination, because of its low purchase taxes and generous duty-free allowances. Explorers from Europe took home exotic foods like peppers, tomatoes and kidney beans, giving Europeans the ability to make a passable vegan chilli for the first time in their history.

Flamboyant Spanish explorers wisely headed for the more sultry South America where there was gold, silver and chocolate, and people could express their emotions through the medium of dance, leaving harsh North America free for dour English settlers, who were more interested in frowning and enormous collars.

Martin Luther and the Reformation

While European settlers were spreading God's word and viruses in the New World, religion was getting complicated back in the old one.

By the 1500s, many people in Europe were unhappy with the Catholic Church, and this was years before they'd found out about the kiddy-fiddling. They reckoned the leaders of the Church were only interested in money and power and dressing in ostentatious cloaks, like rappers. Although that's probably not the comparison they'd have used at the time.

Things came to a head in 1517 when a German monk called King Martin Luther wrote down all the issues he had with the Church, in an early version of Trip Advisor. He wrote 'The Ninety-Five Theses', a very long and self-righteous sort of rant, calling out the Catholic Church. But with no X (formerly 'no Twitter') to post it on, he ended up nailing it to a church door instead. This made the Church leaders furious, because they'd just had it painted, and it had a 'No Junk Mail' sticker on it. As well as a 'No Monk Mail' sign.

Luther was thrown out of the church quicker than a masturbating tramp, but his protest divided the Catholic Church in two – into Old-School Catholics versus the angry 'Protest Ants'.

This split in the Church was to prove very useful for an English king who was something of what we would now call a serial mahoganist . . .

Britain in the Renaissance

HENRY THE ATE

By now, England had got through loads of kings because of a war about roses. These days people think it's mad that we had a war about roses, but my dad almost throttled a man who tried to cut down his wisteria. It's still going through the courts.

When Richard the Third was killed in a fight in a car park in Bosworth Field, the war of the roses came to an end. The war was won by Tudor Henry, who grew a Tudor Rose, and he then passed on the thorny crown to his son, Henry 8, the ultimate nepo baby.

Despite his name, Henry the Eighth had six wives, which sounds like the premise for a very funny farce, but he only had them one at a time, and most of them he killed or divorced. So not the sort of thing that's laugh a minute. The Pope didn't approve of all these wives, so Henry ditched the Pope and all his finery, and made himself head of the new streamlined Church of England. He could do what he liked, and sort it out with God later, because they were best mates now.

HENRY'S HEIRS

Henry eventually ate so many banquets and stood with his legs so far apart that he exploded and died, meaning his young son Edward suddenly became king, aged only nine years old. It's hard to imagine a country ruled by a nine-year-old boy with unbelievable power. He must've been like a more mature Donald Trump.

He was followed as king by Lady Jane Grey who ruled the country for nine days – slightly longer than Liz Truss. After Jane came HMS Queen Mary, who burned Protest Ants at the stake. That must have been fiddly, tying their six little legs to the burning pyres.

THE ELIZABETHANS

When Mary died, it was time for Queen Elizabeth, named after the Elizabethan Age, which had just begun. Elizabeth's reign was the pinnacle of the Tudor era – named after the type of cottages they built – and it became the first great age of entertainment. It seems incredible to think now, but in Tudor times people went to see plays for fun, and not because they were doing them for A-level.

England decided to have a written Renaissance rather than a painted one, because there wasn't so much to paint in England and the weather wasn't good enough so all the pictures went streaky in the rain. And the biggest writer of the age was, of course, measured by output rather than mass, the man who is the subject of the next section, and the question is, do I name him in this bit or do I just do a sort of dot dot dot, knowing that his name will be the next one? Yes, I'll do that, that man was . . .

SIR QUILLIAM SHAKESPEARE

Elizabethan quill-wobbler Shakespeare is one of the most famous writers in the world, alongside Lee Child and Roger Hargreaves.

Shakespeare is such an important writer that I have made my own show about him, *Cunk On Shakespeare.* It's available to view now on an unofficial upload on YouTube that's been viewed half a million times and I don't see a penny of that.

Shakespeare's works include some of these: *Romeo and Juliet, Macbeth, Twelfth Night, Othello, Much Ado About Nothing, Fast and Furious 6* and *Macbeth.* All of which have been turned into films. Which is how we know about them today. Shakespeare had hit after hit after hit with comedies with no jokes in, like Adam Sandler does.

ENGLISH EXPLORERS

While Shakespeare was exploring man's inner psyche, some Brits were actually exploring the real world. The first British explorer was St Walter Raleigh. Raleigh became the darling of the nation by crossing the Atlantic, trading with the Native Americans, or 'Red Indians', as they preferred to be known, and bringing back a potato. It was the worst holiday gift in history. But to be fair, history and holidays had really only recently got going.

But Elizabeth's toughest sailorman was Sir Francis the Drake. He was good at sailing *and* fighting, basically a Tudor Popeye. Drake's ship was *The Gold'N Hind*, which means 'golden arsehole'.

Olden-days boats weren't comfortable mega-yachts like Russian oligarchs and the Duran Duran have. They were little more than ocean-going wheelbarrows. But The Drake and his sailor mates used them to steal gold from more sophisticated Spanish seafarers. The plundering Protest Ant pirates made Catholic King Philip of Spain furious and so he sent a fleet to invade England – The Spanish Armada. Drake and the British fleet won by attacking at midnight – when the Spanish had just finished their lunch and were all sluggish from paella.

JAMES I

Although Elizabeth was the Queen Ant of all the Protest Ants, and could lay eggs, she sadly never did. She left no heirs, which was the olden word for children, making her the season finale of the Tudors. The crown passed to James the Sith of Scotland who now became James the One of England and Wales too.

The nation was now a supergroup of all the best the British Islands had to offer, like McBusted. Britain had teamed up at last. And it was ready to rumble.

THE GUMPOWDER PLOT

James was Protestant and knew that Catholics wanted to kill him, so he had all his clothes padded in case he was stabbed so any would-be assassin would need to use a really long, sharp knife. Or stab him in the face. Or blow him up, which is what the Catholics eventually decided to do.

Today we call the Catholics' plan the Gumpowder Plot, and it's one of the seven basic plots of all films.[*]

The Gumpowder Plot was an attempt by a group of Catholics to blow up the King during the State Opening of England's Parliament. They knew that such an event would make headline news, because engravers would be at the ceremony, and could capture the event live.

---

[*] These are: Hunt for Treasure, Hero's Journey, Looking for Love, Mission to Moscow, Gunpowder Plot, Spice World and Tokyo Drift.

THE THIRD CHAPTER

The Gumpowder Plot plotter we all remember remember is Pennyforthe Guy Fawkes. Guy Fawkes was the Lee Harvey Oswald of the Gumpowder Plot, in that he should be played by Gary Oldman in the film of it.

Fawkes famously smuggled gunpowder into the basement of the Houses of Parliament on the 4th of November, the most memorable date in the history of British bangs. The next night, against all the rules of firework safety, he returned to light the blue touch paper and was caught red-handed, a common injury on fireworks night.

Guy Fawkes was the first victim of extraordinary rendition when he was tortured to reveal his co-conspirators. They put him on the rack and stretched him, presumably until he was then so tall he couldn't fit in any more basements as a preventative measure. It was a tough choice for Fawkes: say nothing and be yanked in two, or cough up names and only be cut in half. He was in pieces about it.

These days we still remember Guy Fawkes every year, when we celebrate Halloween. And to this day, it's traditional to watch the State Opening of Parliament to see if anyone gets blown up.

There are theories that the government knew about the Gunpowder Plot or even masterminded it in order to increase persecution of Catholics. If true, it would have been the first false-flag exercise, and the dark web of the day would have been filled up with theories about it. But there was no dark web in the 1600s, just dark and webs.

IMMERSIVE HISTORY: THE TUDORS

1. You are a Tudor peasant before the invention of the potato – what are you having for dinner?
2. Alternative reality: Henry the 8th is alive in the present day. Where would he buy his clothes?
3. Write a Shakespearean tragedy. Use both sides of the paper if necessary.
4. Research your family tree to see if you are related to Richard III.
5. Invent a sort of 'Tudor' toothpaste by writing the word 'Tudor' on your toothpaste tube in marker pen.

GUY FAWKES

Or literally any man, 1350–1900. Especially Rasputin.

Chapter Four
The Enlightenedment

1620–1660something

With the Renaissance-level 100 per cent complete it was time for the Age of Enlightenment level, which was basically the Renaissance level again but at twice the speed. Philosophers, scientists and economists all exchanged exciting ideas, at what could have been a very boring party, but was actually funny because they all had those mad wigs on.

NEWTON AND AN APPLE

If an apple dropped on my head, I'd be fucking furious – how did Newton keep his cool and invent gravity? That's why he's considered a nearly genius.

Galileo

Galileo was just a poor boy from a poor family. According to Wikipedia, he was 'The father of Observational Astronomy, Modern Physics and Scientific Method'. You'd think he could have thought of better names for his kids.

In the 1600s, this Italian scienceographer constructed a powerful telescope. He didn't invent the telescope, but improved upon an existing design, giving it better lenses, and an eyepiece that you could use to give the unsuspecting viewer a black eye. But it is in his work in astronomy, rather than practical jokes, that Galileo is most remembered.

Galileo used his telescope to wind up the Catholic Church – probably by using it to look into heaven and watch God getting changed, like some Renaissance pervert. Galileo's new telescope left absolutely nothing to the imagination when looking at heavenly bodies. But sadly it wasn't strong enough to see through time. If it had been, he might have been able to avoid a fate worse than shit. His problems started when he used his new telescope to prove that the earth went round the sun, which was directly at odds with the teaching of the Catholic Church, which locked the big G up in his own home. Today, thanks to the teaching of Vanessa Williams, we now know that, sometimes, the sun goes round the moon.

Galileo got the last laugh. Over three hundred years later, in 1992, the Vatican finally admitted Galileo had been right all along, by which point he'd been totally killed by the passage of time. It was the perfect murder.

Saint Isaac Newton

Galileo may have died an idiot, but his science didn't die with him, and over the following decades, a whole generation of eggheads thought up clever-clogs theories using their brains, then wrote them down so normal human beings could read and fail to understand them. One of these sciencebots was St Isaac Newton, the inventor of gravity.

Newton was a mathematician, astronomer and physicist; without St Isaac Newton there would be 25 per cent less questions on *University Challenge*. In one of his early experiments Newton used a prism to split white light into a rainbow, making possible the work of later scientists like Floyd Pink.

But gravity was his killer app. The story goes that Newton was looking at an apple floating in the air. Greedy Newton thought it would be better if the apple fell to the floor where we could pick it up and eat it, so he invented gravity – and it's been with us ever since. It's amazing to imagine that if he'd been three or four feet taller, maybe our world would be very different.

He wrote a breathless account of the event in a bestselling book – the first to be published under the laws of gravity. Previously, any books you dropped simply floated up into the sky and were lost for ever. Now, thanks to Newton, knowledge stayed at your feet, where it belonged.

Gravity changed *everything*. Suddenly so many things made sense – like why dead people fell on the ground. After Britain introduced gravity in 1666, other countries slowly followed suit, with the US state of South Carolina the last to do so – things were still floating around in some counties there as late as 1976.

In recognition of Newton's invention, to this day we eat apples and stick rigidly to the rules of gravity.

Des Carts

The discoveries of Galileo and Newton led to an era of thoughtful thought known as the Enlightenment. One of the least thickiest of the Enlightenment thinkermen was French oeuf-tête René Des Carts, literally 'René of the Carts'. He was a philosopher and a mathematician, and as a result people tried to avoid sitting next to him at dinner parties, sometimes leaving him in his carriage and not even letting him in, hence the name.

With lots of time on his own to contemplate stuff, Des Carts ended up thinking about thinking itself, going right up his own brain's arse, and famously declaring '*Cogito, Ergo Sum*', which is Latinese for 'I think, therefore I am'. He was saying thinkers only existed while they were thinking, immediately throwing into doubt the existence of other philosophers on their day off.

As well as Des Carts, many other philosophers might or might not have existed. One such potentially existing philosopher was the most French-sounding man in history Jean-Jacques Rousseau. He claimed that all people were equal, which raised eyebrows at the time, particularly the well-groomed brows of the aristocats. How could ordinary people be equal, they said, when their eyebrows looked like bears' fingers? Today, we like to think everyone's equal, although let's face it, if that was true, we'd all be writing landmark histories of the world. And that's just not the case, is it?

Beethoven

The Enlightenment saw a vast improvement in the audio quality of the music available. Beethoven (it's not pronounced like that, but anyway) was one of history's most famous composers, although he didn't know it at the time. He was also one of its most remarkable, because for the final years of his working life, he couldn't hear any of his music – Beethoven was deaf.

His outside ears – the ones that could hear the birds and the dustmen – had packed up. But he also had inside ears that could hear the music he was writing in his head but not out in the real world. A bit like when you go into a shop and they've got their own radio station that you can't get anywhere else. Gap FM or whatever.

His biggest hit was duh duh duh DUUUUUH, which he never wrote any words for – maybe because he was lazy, or maybe because he was better at music than words. After all, his words were in German, which is a right fucking mouthful. For instance, in German duh duh duh DUUUUUH is all one word: duhduhduhDUUUUUH, and already you can't be arsed.

Beethoven's deafness is probably why his music is so loud.

IMMERSIVE HISTORY: THE ENLIGHTENMENT

1. Challenge the conventional thinking of Church and State.
2. Drop an apple on someone's head to prove gravity exists. They'll soon see the funny side.
3. Sit and have a think about things. Try to come up with a philosophy that encompasses all of human experience. Make it short enough to write on a cupcake. Warning: don't stop thinking, or you won't exist.
4. Learn to play the harpsichord and impress your friends at parties in houses that have harpsichords.
5. Watch loads of TikToks in case something on the Enlightenment comes up.

THE ENLIGHTENEDMENT

Britain in the Seventeenth and Eighteenth Century(ies)

THE ENGLISH CIVIL WAR

The new trendy 'woke' Enlightenment philosophies about everyone being equal were to prove dangerous – especially when cut with one of the other big inventions of the age: gunpowder.

In Britain, King James's son Charles 1 hated being bossed around by unelected bureaucrats. Eventually, clashes between the King and Parliament led to the English Civil War. Because it's fought at home, a civil war is cheaper than having a foreign war, and you don't need jabs or have to put your shampoo and toothpaste in a see-through bag – it was kind of like a staycation version of a war.

OLIVER CROMWELL & THE PURITANS

King Charles's opponent Oliver Cromwell won the war, and Charles lost his head. Which meant now Cromwell was king. Except – he didn't want to be a king because it was all a bit too 'la-de-da look at me' for plain-speaking Cromwell.

Under Cromwell's rule, Britain changed completely. No longer did the people have to do what the king said. Now they had to do what Oliver Cromwell said. Which was different. Because he did it without jewellery.

He called his government the Commonwealth, and, to show he wasn't king, Oliver Cromwell deliberately hated all the things kings like. Like feasting and burping and music and throwing chicken legs over his shoulder and all the fun stuff. He was well strict, because Cromwell (named after the Cromwell Road in London, now part of the A4) was one of a growing number of British Puritans, a group who thought that God wanted everyone to be miserable all the time.

Cromwell banned lots of fun things – swearing, dancing, pubs, card-playing and Christmas. He even banned sport, which explains why, to this day, the Commonwealth Games are so rubbish. It was Puritan correctness gone mad. Cromwell's Britain had no frills; it was like Tesco owned Britain. And so after Cromwell died, Britain decided to have a king again and everyone was happy again until suddenly, in 1665, the plague happened. Again.

THE GREAT PLAGUE

In London, anyone who showed any symptoms of plague was locked in a house with their family for days, just like they are at Christmas. It's a horrific thought, especially when you consider they didn't have noise-cancelling earbuds.

At night, men would roam the streets with huge carts to collect corpses. In some sense, they were the first rag-and-bone men, because that's all that was left of plague victims.

Rich doctors, lawyers and merchants fled the city, as they still do every weekend to this day. King Charles II fled to Hampton Court, and then, once he found his way out of the maze, to Oxbridge.

THE GRATE FIRE OF LONDON

After the plague came the Grate Fire of London. The fire spread from the grate of the blazing oven of a wooden bakery in Pudding Lane, to a wooden match factory, to a wooden tar-and-brazier warehouse, to a wooden gunpowder-and-lantern shop. Nobody could have predicted the fire beforehand.

Whilst modern buildings are made of brick I think, in the olden days everyone in London had wood. Imagine that. Every erection in the city: hard wood. The only hope with this much wood is to resort to pumping by hand. But people's arms got tired, their wrists ached. And hopes of pouring cold water on London's hot wood faded fast.

People raised the alarm. 'London's Burning!' they shouted. 'Fire! Fire!' One by one, each a little bit later than the other, until they all overlapped and nobody could hear anything. Which may explain why the fire spread so fast. Nobody could understand what everyone was shouting about.

People called 999, but there was nobody there: the Fire Brigade hadn't been invented yet. So when the operator asked what service they required, they didn't know what to ask for and just felt stupid as the flames lapped their knees.

There were some upsides to the fire. Being burned alive was a great way to take everyone's mind off the plague. And for once, coughing was a good thing, as long as it was phlegmy and wet and directed at the base of the fire.

PEPYS'S DIARY

The reason we know a lot about the plague and the fire of London is from the diary of Sam U. L. Pepys. A diary is a sort of book that people wrote down what they had done in, before there was Instagram and TikTok. But what's amazing about Pepys is that he kept a diary when he was older than fifteen. And he kept it for longer than four days.

Samuel Pepys's diary is a bit like *The Secret Diary of A Call Girl*, but with less hot sex and more navy administration. Most of us find looking back over our diaries a bit embarrassing, but Pepys's diaries aren't embarrassing, because they don't talk about who he might kiss on a school trip to Lancaster Castle, and because they're about him, rather than about me.

SIR PAUL'S CATHEDRAL

After the fire was blown out by the King, London was extensively rebuilt by Saint Christopher Wren, and his finest achievement was Sir Paul's Cathedral. It's considered an amazing piece of architecture, because it's both a building *and* a church. Construction began in 1675 but it wasn't finished for thirty-five years. Sounds like they had the same builders I did when I got my ensuite done.

The Cathedral is a building for everyone, even though it costs £18 to get in unless you're worshipping. So it's worth pretending you're religious, like politicians do.

Saint Christopher also built a monument to the fire, called, imaginlessly, The Monument. It's in the shape of a giant match with a flame, which feels a bit triggering.

IMMERSIVE HISTORY: THE ENGLISH CIVIL WAR

1. Tour the sites of the Civil War battlefields if they're not too far and you can be bothered. Don't forget to go home afterwards.
2. Try living as a Puritan for the day. Condemn the indulgent to burn in the fiery pits of hell.
3. Visit Sir Paul's Cathedral. It costs £18 to get in unless you're worshipping, so it's worth pretending you're religious, like politicians do.
4. Eat some eighteenth-century food. Like an apple or anything that isn't a ready meal.
5. You are Samuel Pepys. Write a diary entry for a day when you see a squirrel fight a cat.

'DEATH'

I am quite pleased with how this one has turned out, which shows you some good did come out of the Black Death. So it's a shame that it's printed so small in the book; you have to squint to see the rat.

Chapter Five
The Fifth Chapter

1620 again but in America–1815 in France

As we've seen, after the Renaissance and Enlightenment, Europe had undergone a massive cultural upgrade to Europe 0.1.2, and had come out the end with proper paintings and music that was nothing to do with monks. But while the 'Old World' was transforming itself, the 'New World' – America – was starting from Ground Zero. As we shall see in this next riveting chapter of this unputdownable history book you have been given as a present.

THE ELECTROCUTION OF KING LOUIS XVI

Being guillotined in the head had a major impact on your life; afterwards it was hard to get a job, or even a passport photo. And online dating must have been a nightmare without a profile picture.

America: The Early Years

THE PILGRIMS FARTERS

Plymouth, 1620. A group of Pilgrims gather on the dockside. Should they stay in Britain, which was going all ungodly with people playing with hoops openly in the street? Or strike out for a new, more unhappy life in the New World? It was the first Pilgrim's Choice, and where we get the name of the cheddar cheese brand we buy if they've run out of Cathedral City. Or if it's on offer.

Puritans hated anything fun. They were so strict they made Protestants look like Catholics. These Puritans called themselves the Pilgrim Fathers, but despite their get-up-and-go-for-ever, the Pilgrim Fathers were the least fun fathers ever – even worse than your own father. Imagine that.

As Pilgrims they were at their happiest when living the most miserable life, so Plymouth should have been perfect for them. But even Plymouth's notoriously difficult to navigate ring road was too much fun, because it had roundabouts. They wanted to look for somewhere more boring to live. The only thing Puritans enjoyed was not enjoying themselves, which made enjoying themselves impossible, which they really enjoyed. They decided the best place to have no fun at all would be America, because nobody had discovered Disneyland was there yet.

And so these so-called Pilgrim Fathers decided to sail to America to start a new dreadful life. The Pilgrims knew their journey to America would be dangerous: that they might get scurvy or get lost in a storm and starve; their ship might sink or they might fall overboard and be eaten alive by sharks, or drown and be eaten dead by sharks. But they also knew all of that was better than five more minutes in fucking Plymouth.

The Pilgrims left on the leaky USS *Mayflower* for the worst cruise of all time – even worse than that one where the power failed and people were pooing in the corridors. The *Mayflower* had an all-you-can-leave buffet, nothing to see, and the entertainment came from whoever the 1600s version of Paddy McGuiness was. It was literally hell on wheels. On water.

After some weeks sailing, they arrived in Plymouth. It was a disaster: not only were they back where they'd started, but, money spent, they had little choice but to stay. Luckily it turned out this Plymouth wasn't the same Plymouth they'd just left and the whole name was just a zany coincidence.

And so these plucky, tetchy, mean-spirited, small-minded, miserable Brits were the first Americans – which is why America speaks Britishese to this day, even if they have weird extra words like faucet, fluffernutter and asshat.

THANKSGIVING

The New World was edgy compared to cosy Britain, and the Pilgrims' first winter was extremely hard, which as Puritans they couldn't have been happier about. But when they quickly ran out of food, the empty plates were a bit too Puritan even for them. Luckily they were helped by a Native American called Squanto (brother of Tonto). Squanto taught the Pilgrims how to grow corn and where to fish, thereby helping them survive winter, so that eventually, when spring came, they could give Squanto and his tribe terminal plague.

The Pilgrims were so grateful to Squanto they shared a harvest feast with his tribe, a tradition which became known as Thanksgiving, which is still celebrated, apparently by law, in at least one episode of every American sitcom series ever made.

US INTERDEPENDENCE

Because the settlers were English, the area they controlled came to be known as New England, and over the next couple of centuries all sorts of other European countries opened spin-off franchise countries of their own, with imaginative names like New Spain, New France, New Sweden and so on and on. They weren't New in the sense

THE FIFTH CHAPTER

that they had robots and flying cars. They were sort of the same as the old countries, but with coyotes.

When they weren't infecting or killing natives, the European colonists fought amongst themselves, until eventually the thirteen British colonies started dominating the others in North America. But it didn't take long for those thirteen colonies to start resenting British rule. They particularly hated having to pay tax to Britain, which is why, to this day, large US corporations still refuse to pay tax in the UK.

Spotting a tax loophole, the colonists decided that they weren't British any more: they identified as Americans, and as such, could go to war against the people they formerly were, like when someone turns up at school after the holidays with their hair back-combed and insists they're called Blayze now

THE BOSTON ICE-T-PARTY

The war kicked off in Boston in 1773 when a group of rebels headed to the harbour. There they stormed a ship, and in a custom-made protest designed to enrage the British, threw all the tea onboard into the harbour, without adding milk or bringing the harbour to a rolling boil first. If you factor in a refusal to serve biscuits on the side, you can see what an insult it was to the English.

Of course, it probably would have upset the British even more if this had happened somewhere they could actually see it. But before social media, if something happened thousands of miles away, news of it travelled painfully slowly. In fact, some Britons didn't even learn about the Boston Tea Party until just now, reading about it here, on this page. Me, for instance.

THE FOUNDLING FATHERS

In 1776 in Philadelphia, the leaders of the thirteen colonies signed one of the most famous documents the world has ever known: the American Declarisation of Interdepending. The signing of the declaration document was the most important event in American history, apart from when Dunkin' Donuts started.

But the declaration led to war between America and Britain, on July 4th. The Americans who led that war were known as the New England Patriots. They were led by George Washington DC. Britain lost the war and had to give the country back to the people who rightfully lived there, except for the ones they'd originally stolen it off.

With the British defeated, Washington became the first President of America. He set the tone of fair-minded, statesmanlike rule that epitomised the presidency until 2016, when they figured any mad old cunt would do.

Britain left America to make its own decisions, which has, we can now all agree, worked out incredibly badly for them. But eventually the United States would become Britain's greatest ally, rushing to the British people's aid at the end of any war that the Brits ballsed up and were going to lose. It's odd to think that if they'd done that in the War of Independence, they'd have had to turn up and shoot themselves. History is full of lost possibilities like that.

> **IMMERSIVE HISTORY: THE BIRTH OF AMERICA**
>
> 1. Read a book about the history of the birth of America.
> 2. Write a limerick that starts: 'There was once a Puritan called Tucker'.
> 3. Have your own 'Boston Tea Party' by throwing some teabags in the bath and not paying your taxes.
> 4. List your inalienable rights.
> 5. Spend some money on products from a US-owned multi-national.

The French Revolution

After Americans had overthrown the British, the French – in a typically avant-garde move – decided to overthrow themselves, in a French Revolution.

The penniless French pheasants were tired of having a king, especially when they kept rebooting the Louis franchise with endless sequels and none of the original cast, so they decided to have a storming of the Pastille.

THE REVOLUTION BEGINS

One day in 1789, life had got so hard on the streets of Paris, the poor actually tried to break *into* Paris's most notorious jail, Bastard Prison, in search of a better life. They got in (remembering to leave the door open behind them, so they didn't accidentally lock themselves up), nicked all the orange jumpsuits and mashed potato, and freed the prisoners, all seven of them. There's no one in there now because it's been demolished, making it the world's only invisible prison.

This was only the start for the revolting French: they toppled King Louis XVI (formally Louis TwitterVI) and invented a thing to get rid of him and his like for good – or at least the annoying top parts of them, where the crown was screwed on – the guillotine.

THE GUILLOTINE

With a razor-sharp blade travelling at high speed, the guillotine was designed to be the most humane method of inhumanity ever invented. The guillotine drastically reduced the lifespan of anyone it came into contact with. The head was separated from the body, but the two parts didn't get separate funerals or graves, which makes sense, because it'd be weird to go and pay your respects to the bit that did all the thinking and smiling, then go and pay separate respects to the bit that clapped and farted.

The guillotine was a sort of mechanised axe murderer,

but on the side of the goodies. King Louis and Queen Marie Antoinette were both put into it, to show everybody how safe it was to get executed by it.

People came in their hundreds to watch public beheadings live, but only because YouTube was still only available in book form. When France had finished chopping the tops off its royals, it started chopping the tops off loads of other people as well. The people's revolution had become a splatter fest, like *Slumber Party Massacre II*, which at the time would have still been a poem.

Napoleon's Europe

One man emerged from the revolutionary terror to control France: he'd decided France wasn't big enough and wanted to build an extension of it into the whole of Europe. That man's name: Napoleon Brandy.

All I know about Napoleon was that he was short. Or is that the other one? Nelson? It must have been annoying to have conquered all of Europe and mainly be known for being on the short side. He should have just forgotten about war and invented stack heels.

Napoleon is also famous for putting his hand in his jacket. Or was that Nelson too? I must look these things up. When/if I have time.

Napoleon is still considered one of the greatest military commanders in history, despite losing the European Finals at Waterloo. He was born a humble high-ranking nobleman in 1769 but would swiftly rise to Emperor Level. Napoleon stands as one of the most influential figures in world history, when on tiptoe. And even when sitting he is considered important. Especially if he's sitting looking at maps of countries he has invaded.

NAPOLEON'S RISE

Napoleon was born on the roughest of the Mediterranean islands, Coarsica. During the French Revolution, Napoleon's rise to the top of the French establishment was rapid, not least because everyone above him kept getting their heads chopped off. Such was the political turmoil of the time, that Napoleon only escaped the guillotine because he was too short to put his head in its hole. If they'd tried, it would just have given him a haircut.

Napoleon was good at war, and in 1799 he staged that most French of rebellions, a coup d'état. (French for 'a cup of that'; note: no please or thank you – *very* French.)

Napoleon overthrew the French Directory (precursor to the Next Directory) to become the ruler of France in an era called The Consulate, named after the menthol cigarettes Frenchmen smoke to this day, whatever the health consequences, *n'est-ce pas?*

Napoleon was famously married to Josephine, whilst his brother was called Joseph. Napoleon was obsessed with Josephs. He probably even used Joseph Joseph kitchen utensils when he was cooking, like I do. They're very good, and if anyone from Joseph Joseph is reading this now, I'd love a new set of nesting bowls.

In 1804 Napoleon crowned himself emperor, and his diminutive size meant it was easy for him to reach the top of his head to put the crown on. As emperor he invented the Napoleon Code, one of the few historic codes yet to be the subject of a Dan Brown novel.

THE NAPOLEONIC WARS

Napoleon formed the French military into a Grande Armée, second in size only to a Venti Armée with an extra shot. He used this army to invade everywhere in Europe, fighting his enemies at a series of engagements: the Battle of Wagram, the Battle of Austerlitz, the Battle of Jena-Auerstedt – huge conflicts that will never be remembered to this day.

NELSON

Napoleon was your typical baddie who liked republicanism and equality and freedom – so it was clear to the British that he had to be stopped at all costs. They'd have called Napoleon a 'Little Hitler' if Hitler had been invented.

Napoleon wanted to impose his Continental System (metric) on our great island nation. But one man who had lost half his tickling ability years before wasn't going to let it happen. And that man was Nelson. Or to give him his full name: Vice Admiral Viscount Lord Whore Ratio Nelson's Column.

To this day, Nelson is Britain's most famous admiral. Apart from Admiral Akbar. And the Admiral Insurance people. When Nelson was fourteen he volunteered to serve on the HMS *Carcass* – which doesn't sound like that optimistic name for a ship. Only later did he get to command the positive-sounding HMS *Victory*.

In 1787 Nelson married a woman called Fanny Nisbet. But Nelson wasn't that interested in Fanny and went back to his boat because he couldn't wait to get his hands dirty with some seamen. During his voyages, Nelson lost an arm at Tenerife and an eye at Corsica. Hopefully covered by his travel insurance, but he may have had to fork out for the excess. Always study the policy carefully.

Nelson's first great victory was against Napoleon at the Battle of the Nile, which has been made into a film with Peter Ustinov as the French dictator and the detective Hercules Poirot. For this victory, Nelson was made a Viscount, because people loved him as much as they do the biscuits.

THE BATTLE OF TRAFALGAR

By 1803 Napoleon was on the verge of invading Britain. But there was one man standing – on a boat – in his way. Nelson.

Nelson met the French at Trafalgar Square. For a long time Nelson just waited, on his column, as he does to this day. Then he sent them scattering before they even got to the gift shop of the National Gallery. But during the battle he was shot by a French sniper. Taken below, he slowly died kissing his faithful crew. It was the most erotic death ever.

Even dead, Nelson was now so famous, that if he were alive today he would have been asked to be on *The Masked Singer*. (I wouldn't go on it, even if they asked me, which they haven't.)

NAPOLEON'S DOWNFALL

Napoleon garlickly shrugged off defeat at Trafalgar and continued to cross European borders without the correct documentation. But when he decided to invade Russia in 1812 he made a lot of mistakes, most notably trying to make the invasion into a musical, which was a complete failure: today, only the overture remains.

It was the turning point of Napoleon's fortunes and in 1814 he was cancelled and he was exiled (formally Twitter-iled) to the remote island of Idris Elba, while his place as leader of France was taken by the Bourbon monarchy, the only royalty to invent biscuits until British King Charles's Duchy Originals. For Napoleon, it was a tragic echo of the biscuity adventures of his great rival Viscount Nelson.

WATERLOO

In 1815 Napoleon gave Elba the elbow and returned to France in time to fight a rematch with the rest of the world at Waterloo. This must have been when Eurostar still went there. There he met a coalition of the Wellington, led by the British in-charge-man General Admiral Lord Sir Duke

Of Wellington. Now more famous for his fabulous booty, Wellington started out as a humble senior English aristocrat and field marshal.

Waterloo was another of Napoleon's musical battles, but it didn't achieve victory until covered by ABBA at the 1974 Eurovision Song Contest. Napoleon was defeated at Waterloo (whereas ABBA achieved number ones across Europe with it, achieving Gold Record status in Denmark, Spain and Yugoslavia), and was forced into exile once more, again unlike ABBA, who were allowed to return to Sweden in glory, eventually being awarded the title of Knights Of Orders Of The Vase in 2024.

The British sent Napoleon into exile on the remote Island of Saint Helena in the South Atlantic. Saint Helena was hard to get to and even harder to leave, and Napoleon didn't have access to travel apps like Rome2Rio or Skyscanner to plan his escape. Even if he did, he would find that Skyscanner's cheapest flights from Saint Helena to Paris take thirty hours with a long stop-over in Johannesburg, and come in at around £814. And that's in economy, and I feel sure King Napoleon would want to travel in Business Class, or at least Premium Economy, which would hike the prices to eye-watering levels, even for the former emperor of France.

But there were no planes in those days so, with there being no point waiting for Rome2Rio to be invented, Napoleon died. Allowing Britain to become the dominant force in worldwide history. At this time.

THE FIFTH CHAPTER

IMMERSIVE HISTORY: THE FRENCH REVOLUTION & NAPOLEON

1. Make a miniature guillotine with some razor wire and a matchbox and condemn Brussels sprouts to death. Watch your fingers!
2. Learn French on Duolingo. Say some things that Napoleon might say. Have an argument with Nelson. Remember not to be French for his bits.
3. Raise a Grande Armée.
4. Have a think about Wellington.
5. Invent a modern dance piece that explores the dynastic rivalries of late-eighteenth-century Europe.

WELLINGTON

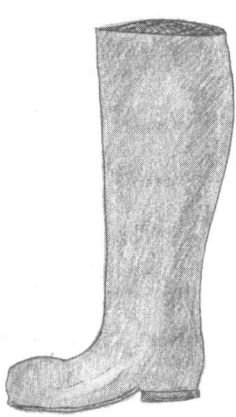

The famous admiral in all his finery. I probably spent too long on this, at the expense of some of the other illustrations, and the rest of Wellington.

Chapter Six
Britain Rues the Waves

BRITAIN 1815–1914

This chapter we're going to look at the time when we reached peak Great Britain. It's a time many British people would like to turn the clocks back to. But they can't, because their clock's digital now and they've thrown the instructions away, even though they swore they left them in that drawer by the sink.

Great Britain. But think about those words for a moment. Great, and, Britain. What do you think of? Beefeaters maybe? Postboxes? The parachute bit in *The Spy Who Loved Me*? These days Brand Britain is one of the most famous in the world. But Britain hasn't always been a trendy buzzword on a slick marketing man's wipe board; it's had to work its way to that position. And the time when that was happening is called *The History of Britain*. And this is that history. As told to you by me, Philomena Cunk, from what I can remember of some of the many history programmes I've made.

In this chapter I show how Britain turned the clock forward to Victorian values, and I'll be asking: why did all Victorian women dress like toilet-roll dolls? And why did the repeal of the Quorn Laws mean there could be meat-free burgers for everyone?

....

ISAMBARD KINGDOM BRUNEL

Or President Abraham Lincoln.

The Steam Age

While the people of America and France were having revolutions, in Britain industry decided to have its own revolution: an Industrial Revolution, getting rid of animal power and thus throwing off the yoke of yokes.

This last and most important revolution was powered by steam. Steam had arrived to teach Mother Nature a long-overdue lesson in God-damn respect. Steam made things bigger, hotter, faster and sexier. It might seem like madness now, but the grey air that hangs around your bathtub actually changed the world.

Steam is like a gas – you can't see it. Well you can see it a bit. But it's mostly sort of see-through and wet. Like a pair of tights.

Steam was invented in Britain, where it started the first Industrial Revolution. Everyone had finally worked out they needed to get out of the fresh air of the farm and spend all day in big noisy steam-filled sheds called factories instead. It was a dream come true.

Steam changed transport too: special wet roads called canals were built, and the steam-powered cow of the future was called a train. 'Trains' could take people wherever they wanted to go, usually to factories. Railways were amazing: they were exciting and fast and in many ways it's a shame we don't have them now.

With all its steam-powered trains and steam-powered factories, Britain became known as the Worksop of the world. Everyone in it was covered in thick black grease, and there were smutty calendars on the back wall, showing women's ankles.

But steam was such an important discovery that Britain couldn't keep it to itself, and soon steam was being exported all over the world. No idea how; they must have packed it in kettles, or maybe they froze it to get it onto the boats. It's a process as mysterious and inexplicable as steam itself.

FACTORIES

Industrialisation created exciting new jobs. Instead of standing in a field waiting for wheat, you could live in your own slum and spend all day in a deafening steel prison pushing a knob in a factory.

These days we all work zero hours, but in the 1800s, workers sweated for long hours in back-breaking positions and had to clean their own equipment, like prostitutes.

People were forced to move to the cities to look for work, where it was probably hiding behind a chimney.

Life was hard in the city. People couldn't even afford bread, just like now when you try to buy a loaf in Gail's.

WORKHOUSES

In order to encourage people to work, the government introduced the Poor Law – which made the unemployed virtual prisoners in workhouses. And that's why it was such a poor law. A workhouse seems like a good idea – it saves time having your work where you live – like working from home. But in fact a workhouse was much, much worse than working from home. Because at the end of the day in the workhouse, you don't get to knock off earlier and watch *Jeopardy!* with a Bahlsen biscuit; instead you work for fourteen hours and eat gruel and sleep three to a plank.

QUEEN VICTORIA

It was during the Industrial Evolution that Britain hit Victorian Times, by having a Queen Victoria. It was an era when Britain would become more powerful, more wealthy and more Victorian than any country on the planet. Victoria married a foreigner, because she earned enough for him to enter the country legally. His name was Albert, or to give him his full regal title, Royal Albert Hall.

It was an era of great engineers and inventioneers. The greatest of these was Isambard Kingdom Brunel. He built a Wapping Tunnel, a Clifton Suspension Bridge and an *Ess Ess Great Britain*, but his towering achievement was the construction of his massive stovepipe hat.

British Art and Literature in the Nineteenth Century

THE ROMANTICS

In the face of the changes to the countryside brought about by the Industrial Revolution, a new artistic movement got invented: The Romantics. Obsessed with the natural beauty of nature's beauty, lots of Romantics were inspired by the beautiful, unspoilt landscape of the Lake District, now reached by the A66 off of the M6. Or you can take the M1 and cut across the Pennines.

Romantic poets were interested in romance. You can still see their work to this day inside the cards people send on Valentine's Day. The Romantics believed that emotions and passion were more important than reason and order – thus creating the most long-running of all boyfriend–girlfriend arguments.

Some famous The Romantics is:

William Wordsworth Common, who wrote 'I Wandered Cloudy as a Daffodil'.

Samuel Coleridge Tinker Taylor, who wrote *The Mime Of Ancient Marina*.

William Blake's Seven, who wrote the theme music for England.

John 'Buster' Keats, who wrote 'Ode To Annie Nightingale'.

And Lord Byron, who started the famous burger chain, after refusing to recognise the Burger King.

Byron and Keats are still greatly studied to this day, because they both died young, and you can read their complete works in an afternoon. It's worth remembering that just because they were Romantic with a capital R, didn't make them romantic not with a capital R. For example, Byron had a baby with his half-sister, which in my book (and this *is* my book) is not romantic at all. But nobody would study the Creepy Poets, so they get to decide their own name.

ROMANTIC ARTISTS

As well as the poets of the age, artists were also getting acute romanticitis. They tried to show the frightening power and beauty of nature, such as *'Hey! Wayne!'* painted by Constable John, the only policeman ever to have painted a masterpiece. The Constable painted a perfect English summer's day: cloudy, and a bit cold; the sort of place where you'd get no service on a phone – one bar at best and that would be 3G. So most serious art historians agree that the Constable could not have sent this picture to his WhatsApp group . . .

J. M. Turnip was another British Romantic painter. He painted lots of pictures of shipwrecks. Turnip did his own stunts like Tom Cruise in the *Mission Impossible* films – he once had himself tied to the mast of a ship at sea in a terrible storm so that he could experience what it was like to be a fucking idiot. Turnip's paintings are considered the most accurate depictions of maritime life until Rod Stewart's 'I Am Sailing'.

MARY SHELLEY

One woman Romantics was arguably Mary Shelley. She was the daughter of Mary Wollstonecraft, the first feminist – she wrote a book called *A Vindication of the Rights of Women* which I really must get round to reading after I've finished this week's *Grazia*.

Mary Shelley is most famous for inventing *Frankenstein* when she was a mere nineteen, only just old enough to see the film herself. The story of the invention of *Frankenstein* is almost as famous as the book itself. In 1816 Byron invited Percy Shelley and his future wife Mary to stay with him on Lake Geneva. Well not on, near. They couldn't float.

They were stuck in their holiday cottage on a rainy day. But unlike holiday cottages today, there wasn't a rack of well-thumbed Frederick Forsyth paperbacks in the hallway, because paperbacks, and Frederick Forsyth, hadn't been invented yet. So they had to write some stories themselves. It was worse than improv.

As a result Mary Shelley wrote *Frankenstein*. Remember, *Frankenstein* isn't the name of the monster, it's the name of the film of the book. *Frankenstein* is all about whether man should play god, but it never says what at. This is all because the holiday cottage didn't have Scrabble.

JANE AUSTEN

Historians tend to agree that another author was Jane Austen Morris, who wrote the first chick lit. She wasn't really a Romantic, despite all her novels being romantic. All of her novels were published anonymously – so even *she* didn't know she'd written them. Incredibly, people still read Jane Austen's books today. Even though they don't need to because all of them have been made into films like *Clueless* and whatever *Bridgerton* is.

Austen's six published books, all successful TV series, are *Sense & Sensibility*, *Pride & Prejudice*, *Edward & Mrs Simpson*, *Rosemary & Thyme*, *Dalziel & Pascoe* and *Walliams & Friend*.

Jane Austen is still so famous she's on the back of the £10 note – to symbolise how much money she has made for other people.

CHARLES DICKENS

Without computers to fiddle with, Victorian people could be bothered to open a book. Perhaps the greatest bookist of his or her time was Sir Charles Dickens. Books by Charles Dickens are sometimes both funny and sad. Hence the expression 'sweet and sour Dickens'.

Charles Dickens most famousist work is *Oliver Twist*. It was originally published in monthly instalments that built up into a fabulous story of a boy who is sent to a workhouse to sing and dance about food glorious food.

Dickens' books have great longevity. They were especially popular in the eighties, when their covers were used to disguise VHS tapes.

THE BRONTËS

Dickens wasn't the only bookweaver in Victorian times. There is also The Brontës.* The Brontës were The Cörrs of their day: three successful sisters and a brother in the background. They all wrote novels except the guitarist. Anne wrote *The David Tenant of Wildfell Hall*; Charlotte wrote *June Air*; and Emily wrote *Wuthering Heights*, which wasn't a success at the time but became a huge hit when Kate Bush covered it 130 years later.

To this day, they remain the most successful Brontë Sisters the world has ever seen (at time of going to print).

Charles Darwin

The Victorian age was an era of innovation and scientific advancement. But one man shocked society with his disgusting discoveries: Charles Darwin.

Darwin invented evolution. Before him, if an animal wanted wings or stripes, they had to ask God. Now, with Darwin's invention, they just had to wait. Ages.

Darwin's ideas were evolutionary, not revolutionary. His theory – and I should explain for anyone reading this in the American South, it is *just* a theory – is about how a man might have once been a monkey. To put it simply, Darwin realised that he had legs and arms and also liked bananas,

---

* Short for Brontësaurus

and noticed a lot of other stuff about animals and worked out that man was an animal too. Darwin proposed that living things change from one generation to the next, like you're probably not as racist as your nan, and all kids are better than you at *Minecraft*.

Darwin had developed his ideas when he went round the world on a Beagle. No photographs exist of this, so it might just be made up. But it's no more hard to swallow than humans coming from monkeys. Maybe he was just testing what people would believe?

If it weren't for evolution, none of us would be here today. Or we would, but we'd be gibbons, and you'd have already eaten this book.

A Crimean War

The Victorian Times were very quiet in terms of war. So they decided to have the Crimean War – which was between Britain and Turkey and Russia. It was the world's first three-way war. I'm not a big fan of three-ways, as it can be quite confusing to work out what's going on, and sometimes it's just easier to sit it out and look at your phone. Which tragically nobody could do at the time.

The most famous battle in the Crimean War was the doomed charge of the light brigade, an event still remembered to this day, in history books like this.

The Crimean War was the first war to have journalists

and photographers on the spot. Before that, the news had to ask members of the public to make tapestries of the event, like at Hastings, and mail them in.

Queen Victoria was so concerned about conditions in the Crimea that she knitted mittens, hats and scarves to send to the front. With hindsight, maybe she should have knitted some bullet-proof vests.

FLORENCE NIGHTINGALE

One woman decided to do something more practical to help in the Crimea than knitting. Florence Nightingale looked after the British injured by inventing nurses. In doing so she drastically cut deaths from infection and created a sexual fantasy that would last more than a hundred years, right up to *Carry On Again Doctor*.

The British Empire

The British had been drawn into the Crimean War to protect their empire. The British Empire was the biggest the world had ever seen. All the pink bits on the map were British. That's because they were ruled by pink-faced British colonists.

Nowadays Britain's main exports are cheese and landfill. But back then the main export was immigration. With the UK population nearing four million, Britain was full. And it was decided to basically have a loft conversion, by converting some of abroad to British.

The British sailed abroad in small boats, looking for bits they could add to Britain. And the first bit of new land they found was Canada's Newfoundland. No one knows why it was called that.

THE DISCOVERY OF AUSTRALIA

In 1788, the first British colony was established at Bottomy Bay. Finally, European explorers had managed to land men on this strange, alien place filled with strange creatures, exotic plants and other people who already lived there, making them the first people in Australia, apart from the First People.

Australia hasn't always been called Australia. It was originally called 'New Holland', because of its distinctive windmills, clog-wearing natives and fields of tulips. And before it was originally called that, it was originally called 'home' by the people who already lived there. Of course Australia couldn't be called 'Home' on maps because that name was already taken, by Britain. When the new Australian flag was raised over the new colony, it had a little British flag on it, to represent how Britain was a long way away now, so looked smaller.

Britain started to send its prisoners to Australia, because it was so sunny and nice with gold lying around and incredible beaches: it was the worst punishment for a British person, because they have nothing to moan about. Eventually Australians had to invent a load of new spiders, otherwise there would be no conversation on the continent at all.

But by the 1870s, Australia was more than a big prison

full of spiders that make you shit your pants. It had its own culture, its own language ('shortening words'), five-day international test match cricket and a mad bloke with a bucket on his head. In short it was every bit as brilliant as Britain, but much further away, unless you lived there. By the end of the nineteenth century, Australians were so proud of their native land that many of them left as soon as they could to travel the world in unsuitable thongs and be mistaken for cockneys by Americans.

BRITISH INDIA

From the 1600s century, Britain traded with India using a company called the East India Company, which got so big, it eventually took over the country. It was a bit like Amazon starting as a bookshop and ending up so big they've probably got an army and a flag.

The East India Company was welcomed at first, because the rulers of India could do business, selling British people 'exotic' and fashionable Indian products, like tea, spices and currywurst sausages.

But eventually the British installed a puppet ruler, called Mir Jafar. The Indians couldn't tell he was a puppet, probably because Jafar was a really good one, like Yoda, and didn't have those Kermit sticks in his arms or ping-pong balls for eyes.

The money that came out of India helped Britain fund things like having an Industrial Revolution, and then insist, hundreds of years later, that giving the Indian people railways was really generous. It was like giving someone the wallet you've stolen off them as a birthday present.

Turning up in a foreign country, taking all its stuff and making its people work for you was Classic British Empire. It was the inspiration for what top industrialist Willy Wonka later did with his Oompah Loompahs, but this was more evil, because there weren't songs.

The British Oompire pretended it didn't really want to take over, but was doing India a favour, which is both quite gangster and really passive aggressive, like a cross between Scarface and an unbearable Nan. If people said the British Empire was ruling India, it said it was just a company, not an Oompire at all, like when my mate Paul refused to answer to his real name at school and said the teacher had to address him as Thugzy.

India suffered terrible poverty and famines while it was run as a company because a country has loads more employees than a normal company, and it's hard for the boss to remember everyone's names, or that they all need lunch. The coffee-break rota alone is a logistical nightmare.

Maybe the best size for a company is 'smaller than a continent and all the people in it'. I can't help noticing that since losing India, British companies have tended to be smaller, like Dyson (the Hoover people), or that woman down the market who makes jewellery out of old SIM cards.

In the 1850s, Indian soldiers serving in the East India Company's army were told that their new rifles would be loaded with sausages, which was against their religion.

They thought it showed that things had gone too far, even though they hadn't minded a tea company having an army.

The rebellion led Britain to crack down on India, and turn it into something called the Raj. Raj is the Hindi word for 'kingdom'. Usually the British got Indian names wrong, calling places like Mumbai something else that they'd made up, so it was quite a concession that they bothered to use a Hindi word and didn't just call it 'Simon' or something.

The British Raj became known as the 'jewel in the crown' of the British Empire, and the British celebrated this by stealing loads of India's jewels and putting them in the Queen's crown back home. This means the jewels can bore British schoolchildren at the Tower of London without them having to travel all the way to India to not be interested.

Late Victorian Authors

SHERLOCK HOLMES

Even late on in the Victorian period, they still hadn't invented TV or Pac-Man, so people had to carry on reading books. And one man they read the books of was Sir Arthur Conan The Barbarian Doyle.

Doyle invented the character Sherlock Holmes, a crime-solving violinist with a funny hat who lives with a doctor. The most popular Sherlock Holmes story is *The Hound Of The Baskervilles*, because it's a creepy mystery story with a dog in it, so it's basically Victorian *Scooby-Doo*.

HAITCHGEE WELLS

While we're doing writers – which we have to 'cause this is an educational book – we can't not mention H. G. Wells. H. G. Wells wrote sci-fi when all science was considered sci-fi.

Wells wrote *The Invisible Man*, about a man who is made invisible so he puts bandages around his face so that he can't hide in women's changing rooms. But HG's biggest hit was the musical *Jeff Wayne's War Of The Worlds*, which is about the chances of anything coming from Mars, which are a million to one, he says, but still they come.

In the musical, the Martians invade Surrey, probably because the schools are better or something, and start blasting people with heat rays, like a sort of evil mobile tanning salon. And then – spoiler alert – the Martians are completely wiped out – by bacteria. They had made a fundamental travel error. They came all that way across space without having their jabs first.

OSCAR WILDE

Another wordsmith in the late Victorian Era was Oscar Wilde. But he put his words in the mouths of actors rather than the ink of the printers. Wilde was what's called a 'closet homosexual', which means he was gay in cupboards but straight everywhere else. One of the people he went in a cupboard with was Lord Alfred Douglas. Alfred Douglas's dad was the Marquess of Queensberry, who invented boxing. Probably not the best person's son to whack off in a wardrobe.

Oscar Wilde was found guilty of indecency. His punishment wasn't that bad, considering he was a literary man – he was given a reading goal. After he was released from prison, Wilde moved to Paris, where it was slightly less Victorian, and he could relax. Which he did, but a bit too much, and he died.

Jack the Ripper

But the biggest mystery in Victorian times wasn't a made-up one, it was a real one – Jack the Ripper. Jack the Ripper terrorised the streets of Whitechapel by carrying out the brutal and horrific murders of five, possibly six, prostitutes. He was so busy murdering he couldn't count.

There's so much we still don't know about Jack the Ripper. To this day, we don't know who he was, we don't know why he did it, we don't even know if his real name *was* Jack the Ripper.

There is still a lot of speculation on the identity of Jack the Ripper. Some people have suggested that he might have been a doctor. But I think that's doubtful, because he's doing the complete opposite of what doctors are meant to do, and would be struck off today.

IMMERSIVE HISTORY: THE VICTORIANS

1. Tell people you are related to Queen Victoria.
2. Watch some steam videos on YouTube.
3. Paint a Haywain. If you can't find a Haywain, try painting a Fiat 500 or similar.
4. Piece together all the available evidence and come to conclusive proof as to the identity of Jack the Ripper. Maybe it's someone you know.
5. Get a mouse mat made with the face of Gladstone on it.

JACK THE RIPPER?

Jack the Ripper experts call themselves Ripperologists, to make what they're doing sound like a science, but it's important to remember that ripperology isn't considered a proper 'ology', like astrology or escapology.

Chapter Seven
Gone West!

America 1800–1914

By now, America was in the middle of the most disruptive case of wandering about grabbing stuff since *Pokémon GO*. Americans believed that the whole of North America belonged to them. And going west to nab it all was their 'Manifest Destiny', which means God told them to do it, the same idea that inspired John the Baptist, The Blues Brothers and Charles Manson.

Americans say God wanted them to take all this land off the native peoples in exchange for spreading democracy and capitalism. God also then asked Americans to spread other stuff, though – like cartoons and iPhones and Papa Johns. (Especially the Grand Slam with Chicken Poppers.) God's generous like that.

....

PRESIDENT ABRAHAM LINCOLN

Or Isambard Kingdom Brunel.

Manifest Destiny

The Americans took their orders from God and got in shitty little wagons and went west, exactly like when they'd got in shitty little boats and left Europe. These settlers would go anywhere if someone said it was better. They were very trusting. I'd rather not risk it, which is why I live somewhere it rains all the fucking time, because I think everyone's still lying about how nice California is. I've seen films, but they can do anything with special effects.

When they arrived at the land God had promised to them, the settlers discovered that it was already rampacked with Native Americans. It turned out these guys had sneakily crept in thousands of years earlier to steal it before the settlers had even been born. It was a sort of time crime.

Native Americans made colonisation hard for the Non-Native Americans, who tried to fill them in about the whole Manifest Destiny business, but the Native Americans weren't having it, and things got a bit tense.

But the new steam engines changed the balance of power. Now, fighting with Native Americans could be conducted on top of steam trains: before trains, if you wanted to fight someone while moving at enormous speed, you'd both have to jump off a cliff and hope to land some decent blows on the way down.

At last, the settlers stood a chance of settling with their brains intact. And settle they did ... in the Wild West.

The Wild West

At the heart of the typical Wild West town was the saloon where you could watch ZZ Top playing some dogs at poker, or challenge a bandit to a duel with gun swords.

Guns played a big part in America at the time, much as they do today. Only the guns then could only hold six bullets at a time, which made it slightly harder to go on a killing rampage, unless you were just trying to kill people in groups of six, say INXS, or Rammstein.

The Wild West was the era of the cowboy and the names from that time are legendary: Billy the Kid, Butch the Cassidy, Wyatt the Earp, The Rhinestone Cowboys, Kid Rock, Sandra Bullock, Mr Ed, Ringo Starr, John Wayne Bobbit, Jessie J, Ned Flanders, Evil Knievel, Crash Bandicoot, Colin Salmon, Wild Bill Beaumont, Buzz Lightyear, The Man from Del Monte, General Knowledge,

Sheriff Omar, Colonel Mustard, Sergeant Pepper, Lisa Left-Eye Lopez, Ben Folds Five, Jon Bon Jovi, Lou Diamond Phillips, Eagle Eye Cherry, Boss Hogg, Doc Who, Billy The Fish, Yosemite Sam, Dennis the Menace, Earthworm Jim, Frank Sinatra and his Rat Pack, William Refrigerator Perry, Flava Flav, Fred Quimby, Ray Parker Junior, the Wu Tang Clan, and Lee Majors or the Six Million Dollar Man as he was known.

COWBOYS

A cowboy was a man (not a boy) who rounded up cows, maybe for questioning or something. Cows might look all innocent and the sort that wouldn't say moo to a goose, but they're just as capable of crime as the rest of us. They're obviously dangerous, for a start, because why else would cowboys carry guns?*

The US Civil War

SLAVERY

America called itself The Land Of The Free. But for many of its population, this meant working for free – because they were slaves. America had been built on slavery almost since its founding: after arriving in America and intending to live a life of honest hard work and toil, the early European

---

* I'd like to see a fight between a cowboy and a beefeater.

colonists had quickly discovered that they couldn't be arsed. So they stole people from Africa.

Working conditions for slaves were pretty basic. There was no flexitime, no paid holiday – not even any *unpaid* holiday. This wasn't just a zero-hours contract, it was a zero-pay contract. And if you did well, you didn't get promoted to superslave or anything. In fact, the career ladder for a slave was almost non-existent. Frankly, the only incentive to being any good at slaving was they'd kill you otherwise. Makes having to piss into a jar in your delivery van look like a fucking picnic.

THE CIVIL WAR

In the mid-nineteenth century, some Americans, mainly in the North, got woke and were beginning to think that slavery might not, when they thunk hard about it, be very nice, and it was actually a bit embarrassing it was still happening. This argument over how racist it was okay to be eventually broke out into a full-on war between North and South. It was called the Us Civil War. Because it was a war between Us, if you were American. It was a seismic moment in American history and to this day American men, who aren't weird at all, like to re-enact it simply to show people the horror of those battles and to get away from their wives for the afternoon.

The Civil War has been described as the first modern war. Partly because they used clever modern things to kill each other, like machine guns and great big cannons on the back of trains; and partly because the North was led by an app, President Abraham LinkedIn. And the South was led by an android, Robot E. Lee.

One of the most famous bits of the war was the Gettysburg Address. Which I've tried to put into Citymapper but it doesn't know it.

After four long years of this sort of thing, the North won, and at last the slaves were free, to be treated equally. Kind of. Slavery was over. Almost. Today's slavery is far more humane, and only really affects children in clothes and phone factories we can't see. And who doesn't love clothes and phones?

The Inventions of the Modern World

Now that Americans had got shooting each other totally out of their system forever, they could concentrate on doing something more positive. So they invented inventing inventions. These were inventions that would change America, and the world – they were the start of modern life. Although still no Nutribullet.

THOMAS EDISON

In 1878, one of the greatest inventors of the age, Thomas Edison, had a bright idea: the light bulb. Suddenly, thanks to the light bulb, all the candles were out of a job. But Edison melted all the unemployed candles down to make wax cylinders, and used these to record sound for the first time, to make the world's first podcasts. Once the light bulb was invented, any time any other inventor had a new idea, they would know, because of what was suddenly over their head. And that ushered in a new age of inventioning.

ELECTRICITY

None of what Edison did would have been possible without the mysterious force called electricity. So I probably should have put this section before light bulbs.

In the olden days, we wandered around looking for food. But now we wander around looking for something else. Electricity. It's literally all I think about: where can I charge my phone?

Before Edison, nobody needed electricity, except for making balloons stick to their jumpers, but now it was out of the electricity bag, suddenly there were loads of inventions that wouldn't work without it.

THE TELEPHONE

Alexander Graham Bell invented the telephone in 1877 and like today, people in the 1870s were staring at their phones – not because they were obsessed with Instagram, but because they'd never seen a phone before.

THE CAMERA

It took the camera to make the phone interesting. Because you can't send a dick pic by voice. You end up just describing the dick and people think that's perverted.

Luckily, the camera was invented in eighteen something or other by someone or other. At first it was rubbish, then it got a bit better; now it's really good and everyone has one. That's basically the story of all inventions.

Suddenly people could see things how they actually looked when they looked at things. It was a revelation. People took pictures of people, horses running, what the butler sawed. Anything that could stay still for three hours.

Another use of film was for photos of a very different sort: X-ray photographs. These terrifying images proved, once and for all, that inside every human being was a spooky version of themselves. Until then, the idea that we all contained skellington monsters was just a nightmare or an episode of *Scooby-Doo*; now that episode of *Scooby-Doo* had become a terrible reality. What other episodes of *Scooby-Doo* might be true? The one with the robot in the old fairground? It's too horrible to contemplate.

And only a few years later, moving films were invented: The Motionies! The first films were made by the French and were unintelligible and weird, establishing a tradition the French have continued to this day.

THE PLANE

Now that phones could connect people miles apart, and films could show us what the moon looked like, it seemed that technology was making the world a smaller place. But it wasn't: the only technology that can do that is an enormous space-based planet-crusher, something that thankfully no one has the will or the money for yet, even the tech billionaires. What was really needed to bring people far apart closer together was something man had dreamed of for many years: human flight.

Humans had dreamed of flying since before they could even dream of flying, but no one could actually do it because birds refused to give up the secret.

As a result of the birds' silence on the matter, men had been trying to fly for a long time: early pioneers of flight are remembered today for providing the backdrop of hilarious bloopers set to early house music.

Someone had to crack it, and it turned out the right brothers for the job were the Wright Brothers.

The Wright Brothers weren't scared of flying, because up until then there hadn't been any films about plane crashes. And so the Wright Brothers managed the first human flight in their aeroplane, called *Flyer*. This plane worked, unlike their previous prototypes *Crasher*, *Exploder* and *Burster Into Flames*.

That first flight only lasted twelve seconds, although the Wright brothers still had to be there sixty minutes before take-off to check in. The flight was so short, the in-flight movie had barely got started. Luckily it just showed a train pulling in at a station, and everyone was walking really fast, so they probably just missed the ending. I won't give it away now, because: spoilers.

Now that dream of flight was and is a reality. Until aircraft emissions destroy the planet and there's no earth for planes to land on.

THE AMERICAN DREAM

But the biggest American invention, bigger than light bulbs or phones or wax-cylinder pornographs, was the American invention of the American Dream.

The American Dream was that anyone could pitch up in the United S of A with nothing but their bootstraps, and if they pulled themselves up on them, they could make millions. All while still asleep. It was a dream come true.

Pitch up they did, from all over. America grew rich and strong and some of the other countries started licking America's arse, like France did when it gave them The Statue of Liberty – designed to welcome new immigrants when they chugged into New York. It's a sort of sexy lighthouse, or 'LILF'.

And the American Dream was certainly a lot more appealing than the nightmare about to unfold in Europe . . .

IMMERSIVE HISTORY: AMERICA IN THE 1800TH CENTURY

1. Give yourself a cowboy name. Your cowboy name is your name with the word 'Wild' before it.
2. Discussion point: if the American Civil War was happening today, which side would you be on? North or East?
3. Make a salad you think they might have eaten at Gettysburg.
4. You are Thomas Edison: invent a sort of electric hat stand.
5. Look at a horse.

THE TELEPHONE

Very much the internet of its day.

Chapter Eight
World Wars 1–2 Inclusive

The World 19.14–19.45

Planes and trains, phones and something that rhymes with phones which I will write in later, had all made the world a smaller place. But they had also made the world a more dangerous place; whereas once you could only fight someone if they were in swinging distance, now anyone anywhere in the world could become your enemy. New technology meant you could phone someone anywhere in the world, call them a cunt, and then watch a *Mickey Mouse* cartoon whilst they flew over you dropping bombs. Millions of new enemies were only a telegram away, and bombs were click-and-collect, delivered in minutes. The era of the world war had arrived.

But there were other struggles in this era too: the battle of the sexes being just one, but the one I'm mentioning now because the next bit is about that.

....

HITLER

The Führer in happier times.

Suffragettes

It is the year 1901. The 1900s are over, and a new century, the 1901s has begun: an era which begins with the death of Queen Victoria, the woman who single-handedly invented being Victorian.

But while Britain had celebrated having a woman king, the thought of having a woman Member of Parliament was vomit-inducing: women could not stand for Parliament any more than they could stand for the toilet. And if a woman had tried to become an MP, maybe by wearing a false beard and burping, nobody would have voted for her, because women weren't allowed to vote, or burp for that matter. It's amazing to think that a mere hundred and something years ago, I wouldn't have been allowed to vote in an election, even though I'm on the telly.

Some women, called suffragettes, decided that had to change (for all women, not just me). To begin with, the suffragettes were basically terrorists – not bad terrorists, like the IRA, but good ones, like The Pogues. One suffragette even threw herself under the King's horse, to protest about how the first-past-the-post system favoured horses.

Many suffragettes were sent to prison, where they tried to starve themselves but were shamed into eating, a bit like the *Mail Online* does to women now, but in reverse.

Fortunately, in 1914 Germany came to the women's rescue, by invading Belgium. Suddenly all those furious women had something to do: world war.

World War at One

Technology in the early twentieth century was advancing at a tremendous speed. But all this technology had a bad side: it could be used to kill people. And not in a good way, like *Duke Nukem 3D*.

The reasons the First World War started are very complicated, and I'm not going to get into it with you here. Not because I don't get it. I totally get it. I just can't be bothered.

Oh, all right then.

The First World War was started by the killing of one man. Frank Z. Ferdinand. His assassination triggered a series of secret treaties, and soon the whole of Europe was taking sides, and getting tooled up, and jonesing for the barney to end all barneys. (Spoilers: it didn't.)

Britain had promised Belgium it would help out if anything awful happened there. So when Germany invaded

Belgium in August 1914-hundred, the British had to act. And how they had to act was 'like they gave a shit about Belgium'.

Britain had made a promise. So it stuck to its guns. Literally. Britain joined France and went to war with the Germans. If Britain hadn't gone to war, Belgium would have just disappeared, and it's impossible to think of Europe without Belgium. No buns, no fruity beers, no Hercules Poirot – it'd be like living under the Taliban.

NINETEEN FORTEAN

Lots of men got over-excited at the thought of this war. The last war had been in Africa, and that had meant jabs. But this one was just over the Channel, so you could pick up a winebox and a flick comb on the way back.

You only have to look at international football matches to see how much the young men of Britain love to go overseas and fight for their country. And the declaration of war was like the European Cup and the Europa League and the European Cup Winners' Cup all rolled into one. Men queued up to fight, confident that it would all be over by Christmas, which in those days didn't start in early September, so that gave them ages.

ALL QUITE ON THE WESTERN FRONT.

But had they known what they were in for, they probably wouldn't have been so keen. The front was awful, like the one at Skegness. Nobody could move. They lived in trenches, which are sort of open-air tunnels, and kept themselves amused by playing the harmonica and growing barista moustaches. It was hell on earth.

The soldiers who'd signed up with such hope in their hearts found the war grinding on longer than a Netflix drama they'd gone off but had to stick with because apparently it gets good by Season 7. It was called 'Attrition', which to be fair does sound like a Netflix drama that gets good by Season 7. It's not like they weren't warned.

All over Europe, countless young lives were lost in fields of mud, noise and confusion. It was like Glastonbury, but working-class people were able to go. This mud wasn't fun mud. It was war mud. The mud to end all mud. It was the mud of the First World War. The worst mud the world had ever seen. So far.

The soldiers were armed with guns but they were also armed with upbeat songs like 'Pack Up Your Troubles' and 'Pack Up Your Tipperary' and 'Pack Your Bitch Up'. But it wasn't enough. You can't stop bullets with songs, no matter how loud you sing. And they died. In the mud. In their millions. In France. In the end. In the First World War. In the past. In black and white.

ALL QUIET ON THE HOME FRONT

Back home in Britain, the war with Germany meant anything German was treated with suspicion. Sausages had to carry passports, and even the German royal family had to pretend to be English, which they have been doing ever since.

Even for ordinary Britons who weren't secretly German, life was hard. It was hard to get food, so the government brought in ration cards, which were no replacement. They were bland and tasteless and made terrible gravy.

To preserve supplies, laws were brought in banning ordinary people from buying the strangest things. You couldn't get fireworks, ruining November the fifth, or buy binoculars, meaning you couldn't see any of the few remaining displays even if they were up the road.

It was a dismal time. You could either go to war and be gassed in a ditch, or stay at home and be cruelly starved of binoculars.

Information was hard to get. The echo chamber had not even been invented, so if you did want news, you had to get the same news as everyone else, in paper form. Or go to the cinema. TikTok and Buzzfeed were rationed so strictly that they might as well not have existed, so if you wanted a hot take, you had to make it yourself, over a gas stove, out of your ration card.

THE RUSHING REVOLUTION

At the start of the twentieth century Russia was a vast empire covering one sixth of the earth, like Pret A Manger does today. It was one of the most important countries in world history, even though I haven't mentioned it yet and I'm 40,000 words in.

Why is Russia so easy to overlook? Most of Russia is very cold and all of it used a very unworkable alphabet unusable for all but the very rich, who could afford to purchase different letters.

In the early twentieth century, most people in Russia were pleasants. But they didn't want to be. They wanted to be unpleasants. The Russian people wanted a revolution – everyone else had had one so why couldn't they? They wanted to vote for their leader. So they voted for communism and then, that sorted, never voted again.

And after waving the red flag, the Russians waved the white flag and dropped out of the First World War: it was so awful that they just gave up and wouldn't play.

ARMISTICE

Fortunately, as planned, at 11:11:11:11:11:11:11, the war ended. It had swept countless ordinary people up into frenzies of nationalism and hatred, wasted the potential of millions of young lives, and left only anger, devastation and confusion. It was very much the internet of its day.

REMEMBRANCE

The war inspired a lot of poets. When you read it today all you can think is – what a terrible waste of life – to have spent it all writing poetry.

Today, we still remember the war on the same day, by looking through old coat pockets trying to find the poppy we bought last year.

> ### IMMERSIVE HISTORY: WORLD WAR ONE
>
> 1. Dig a trench. Ask the land-owner's permission first.
> 2. Write a war poem that rhymes 'church spire' and 'barbed wire'.
> 3. Have a screen-break for five seconds to consider the senseless waste of human life in the First World War.
> 4. Make a 'World War One' pie containing your favourite foods. Use left-over pastry to put the letters WW1 on the top of the pie. Make sure you put a hole in the top of the pie to let steam escape.
> 5. Sign a secret treaty with the Austro-Hungarian Empire.

Women Get the Vote

The war had changed things for women. They started to get the vote; in Britain in 1918, over thirty women were given the vote. And in 1928, over eighteen women. It's not a lot of women, and it seemed to be getting smaller, but it was a start.

Now that women had the vote they didn't have to dress like your nan's sofa any more; they wanted to be treated as men's equals, and do the things men did. They wanted to be allowed to smoke and drink and play golf and party and wee standing up. And so the flapper was born, named after how you dried your skirt if you tried to wee standing up.

Flappers were the Spice Girls of their day. They were all about the look, and all about the nightlife. Now they had cars they could drive to parties, where they could dance the night away with a cocktail and a cigarette on the end of a sort of straw. They wore shorter dresses and hairstyles than before, and liked jazz, back when it was just harmless good-time music you could do the *Bugsy Malone* dance to, and before it became all smart-arsed noise for people in turtlenecks.

The Twenties

The Allies had won the war, but at what cost? For some lucky people, that cost was a profit. Which is clever accounting. Because some people had done better out of the war than others. While millions had drowned in mud or been gassed, others had made a fortune from things that were used in war, like bullets, or blood.

These profiteers became millionaires through a simple mix of canny investment, sharp business sense, and already being millionaires anyway. For the wealthy, the powerful, the aristocrats, life had never been easier. Though it had been *exactly* as easy.

It was the age of the foxtrot, the tango and other dances based on the phonetic alphabet. In the cocktail bars and jazz dives, everyone knew that the war to end all wars was ended and that the best thing to do was get smashed before the next one started.

CINEMA

But most people couldn't afford to have a roaring twenties, so they had to have a boring twenties, like I did, temping in Leytonstone. But they could still enjoy all the fun, at the newly invented cinema and on the radio. Like I did.

Cinema was in its infancy: imagine that you had to get the bus to YouTube, that's how primitive it was. There was no sound on the films, but you still couldn't hear your phone, because some idiot was playing piano. The piano was to distract you from the fact that films had words on the screen, like Scandi detective dramas, which you had to read, or nothing made any sense.

But before too long they figured out how to do sounds too; they called films with sound 'talkies', a name we still don't use today. The first talkie was *The Jazz Singer*, so it was more of a singie than a talkie.

RADIO

Radio, like a virus, is airborne. But you can't catch radio, and there's no vaccine for it, which is why you don't see people wearing masks in the same room as a radio.

Radio created countless stars who we can't remember today. People who became our friends just by talking inoffensively about stuff and filling up time, like Zoella, or someone you've married.

Macaroni invented radio – and cheesy pasta. We don't

know which he was prouder of, but it was probably both. Ironically though, Macaroni never had his own radio show. Makes you wonder why he bothered inventing radio at all. It's like getting a loyalty card for somewhere you never shop.

When people first heard radio, they thought they were going mad and hearing old-time singers in their heads. They only realised they weren't losing their minds when the Prime Minister came on the radio to reassure them that this was happening in real time and that Britain was now at war with Germany. But that comes a bit later.

PROHIBITION

If the Jazz Age had fuel, which it did for the purposes of this sentence, that fuel was booze. It was booze in the clinking champagne glasses, booze powering the Ford T-Models, booze in the trumpets of the band. So when America decided to turn off the booze tap, the Jazz Age came to a grinding halt. It was like when the drink runs out at a party and the lights get turned on suddenly and you can see what everyone really looks like. Awful. Tragic. Harrowing.

The powerful American Temperance Movement declared that booze was bad, simply because it was the root cause of all violence, crime and poverty. But they never considered the positive elements of booze, like helping British people get off with each other, and making Christmas marginally less suicide-inducing. These do-gooders thought that people could have a nice time just drinking tea, praising God and having mind-blowing but sober sex, with Jesus watching.

The Temperance Movement persuaded the US Congress to bring in a booze ban, or Prohibition. God knows why or how, maybe they were all drunk. Prohibition means that they were Pro-inhibitions: they wanted people to be sober and thus shy. The Temperance Movement had finally got its way, but sadly had no way of celebrating its victory.

America had banned booze. But Americans still wanted booze. Even more so now that it was banned. Like, they banned Deeley Boppers at my school, and of course everyone then wanted Deeley Boppers. Then they banned flick knives, and of course everyone wanted a flick knife. Then they banned heroin, although actually I think that had always been banned.

SPEAKEASIES

Prohibition created a black market for booze. Which is like Black Friday, but every day of the week and only for alcohol. People would go to secret bars called speakeasies that were often hidden behind other premises – diners, shops, undertakers, other speakeasies. Chicago boasted a 'speakeasy' centipede of seventeen speakeasies, each more debauched than the last. People were walking into speakeasies and drinking cocktails when all they wanted to do was pick up their dry cleaning, and so Prohibition was making people drink more: the very opposite of what it was intended to do.

GANGSTERS

Making a mint julep (clever!) from all this boozing were the gangsters who ran them. People like Alan Capone, John Dillinger, Busby Malone, the Greek Gatsby, 'Dutch' Elmdisease, Al Pacino, Machine-Gun Edmonds, Tony Soprano, the Notorious BIG and Def Leppard. These were men who would solve a problem with a gun, especially if the problem was: how am I going to get this bullet in your eye?

The most notorious mobster was Chicago's Alan Capone, who was also known as Scarf Ace, because he had the best neckerchief in the tri-borough area. He was the mastermind behind 1923's St Valentine's Day Massacre, which saw seven men dead after Capone saw the price of a bunch of roses on February 13th.

By 1933 everyone was parched from the violence and they decided everyone needed a drink. Prohibition was itself prohibited. Cheers!

EINSTEIN

Despite all the jazz coming through the walls of their laboratories, scientists were also absolutely smashing it in the 1920s. Physicist and Mr Marilyn Monroe Albert Einstein came up with his Theory of Relativity, $E=mc^2$, which to this day nobody understands and I'm only mentioning it now because it turns out to be important later.

ALEXANDER FLEMING

Penicillin was the first handy biotic, discovered by a Scottish man called Alexander Fleming. He found that mouldy dishes would kill disease, which is the actual opposite of what your mum tells you when she visits you at college. But that's probably why nobody ever gives your mum a Nobel Prize.

Antibiotics would revolutionise medicine. Today they form the backbone of the fight against infection, and will probably do so for weeks to come.

FREUD

Like Einstein, Sigmund Freud was also a German-speaking boffin – but a new sort of boffin: a pervert boffin. He wanted to explore the workings of the human mind, and to do that he had to lie people on couches and ask them all sorts of pervy questions.

Freud was technically the nosiest person who ever lived. Freud called his technique psychoanalysis, which is the medical term for perving. He said that by understanding what, if anything, went on in people's minds, you could understand human behaviour. Plus he gave us the word 'anal', so his legacy lives on in hundreds of websites to this day.

Freud decided that the human mind was divided into three bits: the ego, the superego and the ID. Basically, the ID is the economy-class bit of the mind, the superego is the business-class bit, and the ego is the sort of economy-plus bit of the mind – so the ego gets free pretzels and slightly more leg room, but still has to use plastic cutlery.

I should really have talked about Freud earlier, before the First World War, but I couldn't find a good way of fitting him in. History's messy like that; things sometimes don't happen in the order they should to make for easy reading.

Britain's General Strike

But even with all the jazz and science and psychoanalysis, things weren't looking rosy. The world economy was in a right pickle, and many industries found it almost impossible to sell their goods abroad – even pickles – because abroad was mainly rubble.

In Britain, the coal industry was badly affected. Coal is a sort of bricks you can set fire to, and it comes from under the ground, where it was hidden by dinosaurs for winter.

The miners who hunted for coal wanted to be paid more money in return for spending all day miles underground in the dark being crushed by rocks. But the people who owned the mines didn't want to pay them because they thought the miners were living underground rent-free, like Wombles, and should be grateful.

In 1926, the miners stopped working. Not like when you stop working because you want to look at Twitter for a bit, but they stopped working *and* told their bosses that was what they were doing. It was something called a strike.

Soon thousands of workers from other industries joined them. Not in the mines. That would have been horrible and dangerous. But outdoors, standing round a bin on fire. Which is the international sign for being on strike.

After ten days, the miners returned to work having won the right to stay underground for longer for less money.

The Great Depression

If money makes the world go round, then in 1929 the world stopped spinning. But only metaphorically. There was a dreadful crash in New York. It was between a wall and a street, and it destroyed most of the money that was there.

America immediately went into a Great Depression. Hoboes with holes in their hats jumped on trains in big clouds of dust, and Laurels and Hardies roamed the land looking for work on railway pump-carts, and then ballsing it up, getting all soot on their faces, and blinking.

America stopped buying things from Britain. Back in those days, if you had a Hugh Grant or a Hugh Laurie or any posh Hugh to sell, America would have told you to bugger off. Our exports were knackered.

So even though the Great Depression started in American, it bummed out the whole of British industry. Soon two and a half million British people were out of work. Not out of work in the Friday afternoon down the pub sense. But without any job at all, like Prince Andrew.

> **IMMERSIVE HISTORY: THE INTER-WAR YEARS**
>
> 1. Throw yourself under the King's horse.
> 2. Learn an instrument and play some 'jazz'.
> 3. Go on strike.
> 4. Prohibit something.
> 5. Dance a foxtrot with a consenting adult.

World War the Second

By the 1930s, humanity had finally got the First World War out of its system, and now everyone was having a lovely time. So it was time for another war.

World War the Second was even better than the original: faster planes, bigger tanks, more explosions, and it was a bit more obvious who were the baddies. If you want to know more, watch my upcoming landmark fifty-part landmark TV series, *Cunk: A Warning From Hitlery*.

WAR LOOMS

After the tremendous success of *World War I*, a German group called the Hitler & The Nazis decided to start a sequel war – *World War II*. And this wasn't just an opportunistic cash-in: they were determined to make sure it was even better than the first one. It was to be the *Trolls II: Trolls World War*.

THE RISE OF HITLER

It was all started by a Dolf Hitler. The youngish Hitler (probably with an early moustache) was sent to a German Workers' Party, but instead of turning up with some crisps and a six-pack like anyone normal, he just took it over and renamed it the Nazi Party, which should have been a bit of a clue to everyone that things were about to go a bit nanas.

Hitler then staged an even bigger party – a sort of evil carnival – where he and his mates marched through Munich. That was enough for the authorities, who banged him up in prison. And that should have been the end of him, like at the end of a *Scooby-Doo*.

But in prison, Hitler was a bit like *The Very Hungry Caterpillar*, except instead of stuffing his face with lollies and that, he wrote a book called *Mein Kraft*, which was later made into a game with all blocks in it. And when he got out of prison he turned into a Nazi butterfly who was impossible to ignore and had his own distinctive markings.

The headmaster of Germany, a man called Hindenburg, who was named after an exploding balloon, could see Hitler was going to be trouble, so he made him deputy headmaster, hoping this would keep him in his place. But then the headmaster died, and Hitler combined the roles of head and deputy head into one job, called Führer, which is German for 'ultimate end-of-level bastard'.

1939: THE WAR STARTS

Hitler had a brilliant plan to make sure it wasn't going to be one of those 'difficult second wars'. In a plan of incredible low cunning, he spent the 1930s secretly building tanks, planes, ships and armies. And when the other countries asked what he was doing, he just said he wasn't.

In 1939, Hitler blew kick-off on the war and invaded Poland, which he'd promised not to do in 1934, with the 1934 German–Polish Non-Aggression Pact, but it wasn't 1934 any more, so he probably thought it was fine.

The Poles had signed the pact without reading the terms and conditions, which were almost certainly written in that olde knights-in-armour typeface Hitler liked, so very hard to read in small-print form. It was worse than iTunes T&Cs or the bit at the end of an advert for pills where they talk at double speed.

Hitler had long planned to knock through into Poland and make Germany a more open-plan country, probably with a really big table, a kitchen island, and some complicated new bins hidden in cupboards.

Britain and France had promised to defend Poland in the event of invasion, but they were a long way away in – respectively – Britain and France, and so sheer geographic necessity meant the war took a while to crank up.

1940: THE BLITZ

But within six months, France, too, was occupied by the Nazis, and Britain was alone against Germany, like a penalty shoot-out, but with bombs. And in Britain's goalmouth was the safe hands of PM St William Churchill.

Hitler's target was Britain itself. But the Royal Air Force fought back with a Battle of Britain. And as battles go, it had everything. Little planes drawing smoke lines in the sky. Tables covered in little flags that you can push around with fondue forks. Men with sheepskin collars running between sheds.

The Germans were beaten in the air. So they decided to try a different thing instead: the Blitz. These days people associate the word 'blitz' with NutriBullets, but back in *War Of The Worlds II*, it was with real, giant, non-nutritious bullets – called bombs. Many people lost their lives and their homes; places like Coventry, and Coventry itself, were devastated.

1941: THE PEARL HARBORER

Even though it was a world war, for America the war only started when the other baddies, the Japanese, bombed Michael Bay's Pearl Harbor starring Ben Affleck and Kate Beckinsale. Pearl Harbor was a disaster and, with thousands of sailors killed and a Rotten Tomatoes score of just 24 per cent, it was no wonder America came back swinging.

1942–3: TOTAL WAR

War Of The Worlds II was even worse than the first version. This time, mechanisation was everywhere: tanks, radar, flying bombs, flying tanks, flying radar, and a sort of naughty typewriter called the Enigma machine, which could be used to make films about people with glasses.

1944: THE D-DAY

The Nazis had taken so much of Europe over that there was a worry that the only place for posh Americans to come on holiday would be Britain, where it was raining. Something had to be done. And so the idea was invented for a new day, called the D-Day. The 'D' stood for 'D', to make it easy to remember. It was the cleverest code of the war – because everyone could solve it. Adolf Churchill knew that his arch-enemy Winston Hitler was so busy putting codes into his Enigma machine that he wouldn't see it coming: the perfect plan!

The Save The Day invitation said it was going to be June the 1944th, and everyone was ready. D-Day was going to be based on the Nazis' successful invasion of Europe, but backwards. The twist was that the people doing it this time would be the goodies. And the whole thing was based on the video game *Call of Duty*, so the soldiers would be able to practise at home and know where the pick-ups and health packs were.

D-Day happened on a beach in Normandy.

If you watch real-life footage of the invasion, directed by *Jurassic Park*'s Steven Spielberg, it's exciting and award-winning, which is the last thing the Nazis were expecting. Their films were in black and white and about parades and a man on a box shouting.

D-Day is still regarded as one of the best army things ever, by people who collect knives.

1945: THE VE DAY

After six gruelling years, Hitler finally turned his hobby of killing people on himself. And so, with Hitler an ex-Nazi, on 8/9 May 1945, Germany surrendered.

VE Day was a beautiful day. People waved flags, which, to be honest seems risky, as that's also how wars start. But people celebrated surviving by kissing each other and doing dances to black-and-white music. Later on that year there was VJ Day, to celebrate the launch of the vajazzle. It would take fifty years to catch on.

Vajazzle Day coincided with Japan being beaten when America gave it a shock that meant it had to surrender or not exist any more. And that shock was the atomic bombshell.

The development of the atomic bomb was called the Manhattan Project, in which British and American scientists somehow managed to turn Albert Einstein into an atomic bomb. Which is why I mentioned him earlier.

The atomic bomb dropped on the Japanese city of Hiroshima in 1945 exploded with the force of 15 kilotons of TNT, but that won't mean much to you, unless you work in a strip-mine. Einstein exploded, with his hair in the shape of a mushroom and his tongue out. It only took one more epoch-changing bomb to make the Japanese finally surrender. War was over. For a bit.

> **IMMERSIVE HISTORY: THE SECOND WORLD WAR TWO**
>
> 1. Stage a beer-hall putsch. Ask the landlord's permission first.
> 2. Design your own 'swastika-like' symbol. Ask someone to knit it onto a flag. Unless you can knit.
> 3. Invade Poland.
> 4. Carve a potato into your favourite WW2 general.
> 5. Learn to smoke a cigar and pretend to be Churchill for a day.

THE BATTLE OF BRITAIN

Winston Churchill, 1940: 'The Battle of France is over. I expect the Battle of Britain is about to begin . . . if the British Empire and its Commonwealth last for a thousand years, men will still say, "This was their thinnest hour"'. Probably because of all the rationing.

Chapter Nine

The Post-War Twentieth Century

The World 1945–2000

The second half of the twentieth century is an era of wars not involving Germans (for once), and an era of pop music also not involving Germans. Except for Nena and her Neunundneunzig Luftballons.

....

THE BEATLES

Very much the Technotronic of their day, now the Beatles are almost totally forgotten, only popping up occasionally on eight-hour-long documentaries, and four-part biopics.

Post-War Britain

After two world wars, the endless repeats of that Vera Lynn song on the radio had left Britain exhausted and depressed. Times were tight, and there were things Britain could no longer afford, like food, stockings and the Empire. Britain had to get used to being a bit smaller, just the size that it actually was, rather than pretending it was India and Africa too. The great British Empire gradually disappeared, bit by bit, like Christmas cake or loom bands.

Black-and-white movie star and new Prime Minister Clementine Attlee rebooted Britain and gave it a whole new operating system with some amazing new apps, like the NHS and Social Security. Council homes were built, so councils finally had somewhere to live. And children were allowed to stay on at school until fifteen, which is three o'clock in old money.

IMMIGRATION

As Britain got back to work after the war, it realised it was short of workers, because so many of them had been turned into soldiers by the government and then turned into dead soldiers by the other soldiers.

There were houses to be built and hospitals to be staffed and transport to be manned, but you can't do that with dead soldiers because it scares kids, so Britain looked abroad for help, and turned to a country called the Commonwealth, which was everywhere Britain had previously invaded.

And so, in 1948, a boat called *Windrush* brought 500 people to Britain from the Caribbean. These new arrivals were British, and they were welcomed the same way British people welcome any other Britons: really awkwardly, and with bad grace. Life was very difficult for the Windrushers here: Britain was full of people who didn't realise they were racists until they came face-to-face with some people who looked different to them. But this was the start of Britain becoming multicultural, and before too long policemen would be dancing awkwardly with carnival women with all feathers and their bums out, and the national anthem would soon be 'Red Red Wine' by UB40.

THE 1984

In 1949, a book was published that looked at the future and tried to work out just how awful it was going to be. The book, by the thinking man's thinker George Ohwell, was called *1984*, and was set in the year of the same name even though it hadn't happened yet. This was a science fiction book with the emphasis on the word 'book'.

Anyone who read *1984* and tried to put a bet on the future based on what would happen would have lost the lot, because Ohwell got it totally wrong. It was an irresponsible book to publish. In many ways it's not worth reading the book now, because 1984 has already happened and he got it so wrong. Plus there are loads of films of it, and twenty-four series of *Big Brother*, and so it's easier not to see those instead of not reading the book.

The star of the book, Winston Smith, works for the Ministry of Truth, rewriting past newspaper articles so the story fits the party line: a bit like Fox News, except Winston Smith never got sued by a vote-counting company.

CORONATION TREAT

After that burst of the future, being old-fashioned became very fashionable again in 1953, when Britain got a new Queen: Elizabeth the Two. Elizabeth was only twenty-six when she turned into a queen, and she went on to be the longest-reigning monarch in the *Great British King-Off*. There are stories claiming sightings of her in mirrors at Buckingham Palace to this day.

Thousands of Britons watched the Queen being coronationed on their new televisions, even though they were black and white and tiny, as were the televisions. It must have been like being in a leaky caravan during Charles and Diana's wedding, like I was.

People who didn't have TVs went round their neighbours' places to watch Elizabeth getting Queened. Some boasted of watching the event being broadcast over a 'nine-inch Bush,' which gives you some idea of how bad British personal hygiene was in those days. No wonder VJ Day was a flop.

People didn't take the TVs back after watching the coronation. They kept them in their front rooms and never went out again. The TV age was well and truly here. And it would last until the invention of short video clips.

Post-War China

The defeat of the Japanese in WW2 meant that China now had room in its schedule for another kind of war, so they decided to have a civil war between the Nationalists, who weren't communists, and the Communists, who were, as their name hints, communists. The Communists were led by This Chairman Meow.

For years there had been only one flavour of communism: Soviet communism. But then Chairman Meow realised that, as with almost everything, the Chinese could knock off a copy of it without paying for any of the IP. It's something the Chinese still do to this day: if you're reading this in Mandarin, don't think I'll be seeing a penny of whatever you paid for it.

This Chinese Communist knock-off infuriated the

Russian communists, who had hoped to roll out communism all over the world but, since they were anti-profit, they couldn't really complain.

Despite leading the Communists on the famous Wrong March, Chairman Meow won the civil war and in 1949 he proclaimed the Chinese People's Public of China.

Meow wrote his thoughts in a 'little yellow book': what we would call *The Yellow Pages.* He mainly wrote about local locksmiths and plumbers whose names started with AAA. But then he got rid of capitalist companies so there was only one number in *The Yellow Pages* – the Chinese Communist Party. And they were ex-directory.

Charming Meow started to reform Chinese society with the Great Leap Forward, but it was a failure: even after five years, no one could jump more than twelve feet forwards or backwards. So then it was time for Meow's difficult second revolution, which he called the Cultural Revolution, which sounds like it's going to be about some nice new music or mime or something, but actually involved the deaths of two million people for often minor perceived deviations from strict Communist principles.

Today, China has itself deviated slightly from strict Communist principles by becoming the second-biggest capitalist economy in the world.

The Cold War

China turning Communist only added to the dangerous political polarisation of the planet. Earth already had two poles, North and South; it was about to get two new ones – East and West.

The end of double-you-double-you-eye-eye meant that without Germany to mutually hate, communist East and capitalist West now got suspicious of each other. It was the beginning of a whole new type of conflict . . . it was named the Cold War because it was annoying and persistent, like when you can't get rid of a cold.

The planet split into two teams, again. On one side, the West – America and its allies – who believed in supermarkets and Jesus. On the other, the East – Russia etc etc etc – who believed in not that.

SPIES LIKE U.S.

Soon there was so much mistrust and paranoia between East and West they started spying on each other. Russia got so into spycraft, it replaced its entire alphabet with a secret code literally no one could understand.

Spies could be anywhere. They were masters of disguise. One minute they'd be cleverly infiltrating society by sitting at a roulette wheel in a tuxedo, the next they'd dress up as a mole and burrow into the nearest government building. Literally anyone could be a spy. You might've been one yourself – without even knowing. You might be sitting next to a spy now. Whilst reading this book. Who *is* next to you? Yes, it might be your spouse of over twenty years, but how well do you really know them? Where is it they go on Tuesday afternoons? And what's in that box they keep in the spare room? And why were they photographed passing microfilm to the Russian ambassador in St James's Park yesterday afternoon? You could just ask them outright: 'Are you a spy?' But the very best spies are trained not to crack under this sort of pressure.

TWO TRIPES

The Cold War saw a build-up of weaponry, even though the two sides didn't have an open fight to sort out who was best. Instead America and Russia got smaller countries to fight on their behalf, something called 'poxy wars', which is a bit condescending to those doing the fighting. West fought East in a series of compass-defying conflicts: North Korea v. South Korea, and North Vietnam v. South Vietnam. These wars, though bloody, were at least convenient given the proximity of the belligerents: travelcards were accepted on both sides of the border and there was no language barrier to delay the bloodshed.

America joined forces with other Western countries to form a military club called the NATO and the Russians joined up its Eastern allies into the Warsaw Pact, which the Russians claimed was a peaceful organisation, even though it had the word 'war' literally as the first half of its name, and the other half was a horror-film franchise. East and West Europe were divided by the irony curtain, which meant neither side could see when the other was being sarcastic, increasing the danger of nuclear conflict.

The one ray of hope was Berlin where, despite their mutual acrimony, the two sides collaborated long enough to build a magnificent wall through the middle of the city. The mega-wall divided Berlin into East Berlin, and the other bits. It became not just a symbol of global disharmony – but an inspiration to bricklayers everywhere.

THE SPACE RACE

The rivalry between the two sides didn't just extend side-to-side horizontally in a wall, but vertically, into the air and beyond.

During the war the Nazis had invented rockets so they could deliver explosives to London incredibly quickly – like a sort of violent Amazon Prime but with even more probability that the delivery would be left with an unknown neighbour.

But now the Americans and Russians both wanted to be the first to use a rocket to blow up the whole of space and, in 1957, the Russians came first and successfully launched Spunk Ink into orbit. It was a pilotless mission, and so no human had yet set foot in space; over the next few years the head-eggs in charge of the space race were dealt a series of blows when animals beat them to it. First, a monkey called Albert, then a dog called Laika – who also had the incredible honour of becoming the first animal to die horribly in space. At least that's what the history books tell us; I like to think that maybe Laika's still up there now, gazing through the window of her spaceship, staring down at the earth hoping to catch a glimpse of her owner coming to take her for walkies. Hoping in vain. And really hungry.

Slowly the truth dawned on the space scientists: dogs can't pilot rockets very well because their paws don't fit the steering wheel, and most of the ones who survived the initial launch into space ended up sticking their heads out the window and never coming back. Probably thinking the planets are balls and chasing them across the Milky Way.

Humans finally caught up with the animal kingdom in 1961 when Yuri Gagarin went into orbit using nothing more than a massive spaceship. Having orbited the earth, he decided he enjoyed life in Soviet Russia marginally better than the oxygen-less void of space, and returned to our world to live among us once again.

America in the Fifties

While Russia was winning the Space Race, America was winning the Supermarket Sweep, by building giant shops on every available surface. The shops needed some stuff to sell, so factories that had been used to make bombers and jeeps during World War Two were quickly converted to make consumer goods like fridges, hotdogs and, above all, televisions.

TELEVISION

By 1958, 83 per cent of American homes had a TV, even though there wouldn't be anything worth watching until season one of *The Ghost Whisperer* starring Jennifer Love Hewitt was broadcast forty-seven years later. Season two saw a slight dip in quality, only to recover strongly in season three, when the character Paul Eastman was revealed to be Melinda's biological father in a shocking finale that never appeared on 1950s television sets.

ELVIS

One of the first stars of this new television age was J. B. 'Elvis' Priestley, who overcame a hip impediment to become one of the biggest celebrities in history. At the time, his performances were considered so daring and sexy, he could only be shown from the feet up, with all his clothes on, and even then he was eventually sent into the army to calm down.

Elvis's biggest fans were 'teenagers' – a newly discovered species of human who didn't want to wear boring suits and ties and white picket fences like their mums and dads did. They wanted freedom, to rebel without a cause and do the milk-hop at the laundromat in their 501s, drive their Chevys to the levy, whatever that is, and maybe stop off at the drive-in movie jukebox diner on the way home to make out with their sweetheart on prom-night. Nobody knew what any of that meant, which was why it was so rebellious. But the teenagers loved doing it. Whatever it was. And little wonder considering what was going on in the wider world...

The Cuban Missile Crisis

In 1959 there was a communistic revolution on the Caribbean island of Cuba, a country I haven't mentioned yet even though it'd been there the whole time, near the tip of the USA's flaccid Florida.

After the revolution, a man called Fido Castrol came to power in Cuba; he wanted to turn this tropical paradise into a communist wasteland for some reason. Then in 1962 America discovered the Soviets were going to use Cuba as a place to hide their nuclear missiles; at least if they accidentally exploded, they wouldn't be anywhere near Russia.

America was furious and threatened a nuclear telling-off. The Soviet Premier blinked, and while his eyes were closed, Castrol quickly got rid of the missiles. The Free World had prevailed, but the Cubic Missile Crisis wouldn't be the last dangerous Isis the world would see.

The Sixties

Having swerved Armageddon, America could focus on really tucking into the 1960s – a time when young people rebelled against old ideas, and society underwent a series of shocks that would change it forever. Into what it would have been today if things could just stay the same for a bit. Because the 1960s was a turning point in the story of the people of the West, who overnight turned from sort of grey mole-people in bowler hats into beautiful butterfly hippies smoking LSD and playing wig-out music on the kaftan.

America in the 1960s was dominated by the counterculture; counters were everywhere, from cafes to counter wholesalers. Fashionable Beat Poets like Jack Anorak and Allan Ginsburger wrote their Beat Poems on these counters. Beat Poems are poems which reject mainstream poetic values like rhyming or being suitable to read at funerals.

The counterculture was a rejection of all the things that had made America what it is today, if today was a day in the early 1960s. Counterculture rejected the things that most Americans had – until then – taken for granted; things like washing every so often, having a job and not being stoned at eleven in the morning.

The counterculture's rejection of societal norms was taken up enthusiastically by the new hippie movement, who rejected conformity by all wearing the same jeans, growing the same long hair, listening to the same music and smoking the same drugs. Conformity could do one, daddy-o.

Music played a pivotal role in the counterculture. No longer was music just for playing in the background during a cocktail party, or for encouraging consumerism; music was going to change the world, once everyone had slept off the weed.

Fashion, too, underwent a radical change in the 1960s. The boring, beautiful suits and dresses of the fifties were dumped to make way for free-spirited, ugly bell-bottomed jeans. Tie-die was very much in vogue: if you wore a tie you deserved to die. Hairstyles changed: men grew their hair long, so they could wear flowers in it, which is impossible with a buzzcut. You might manage to stick a daisy in a skinhead, but it would fall out as soon as you picked up a placard for the BAN THE BOMB march.

DALLAS, 1963: THE KENNEDY ASSIGNATION

If Cuba had fired missiles at America, it may have worked out better for sixties heartthrob and President Johnneth Kennedy. Because in 1963 he'd have been safe in a nuclear bunker avoiding the fallout rather than driving through Dallas following the latest fashion of not wearing a reinforced steel helmet.

Kennedy was in Dallas to open a new schoolbook depository managed by Lee Harvey Nicols Oswald. But an enraged Oswald, furious that Kennedy hadn't returned a textbook on calculus he'd borrowed, spaffed at Kennedy with a rifle and nicked a bit of his brains out: one of the harshest fines ever issued by a serving librarian. Kennedy's wife, the super-Irish Jacky O'Kennedy, tried to catch his brain blob but it slipped through her tender loving butterfingers.

Kennedy was then shot a second time by local cameraman 'Zap' Ruder, so he could make the world's first bloopers reel. After the assassination, Oswald was himself shot by nightclub impresario Jack 'Your Body' Ruby, while the world looked on in horror.

America was in shock. Like when that guy who played Kramer went racist. Their favourite, and only, President was dead, and questions were being asked: 'Was Oswald the only assassin?', 'Why was it so easy for him to shoot Kennedy?' and just plain 'What the fuck, dude?'

Conspiracy theories soon started to take shape. And the shape they took was a bad one, not symmetrical but nebulous and shifting, like the sort of gas that surrounds the devil when he materialises on earth in old films. It's amazing to think that there even were conspiracy theories before Twitter formerly known as X formerly known as Twitter.

Some said Oswald wasn't the assassin, that he was just a pasty, and that the assassination was really done by the CIA, the mafia, the Cubans, the Nubans, Nice President Lyndonbee Johnson, the Teamsters, the Waltons, the Tates, the Bundys, the Munsters, the Huxtables or even the Brady

Bunch. Some said it was Jackie herself, firing a small gun into Kennedy's chin, back and to the left. *

There were also reports of a second shot fired by a known C&A informant called Grassy Noel. There was also talk of a so-called magic bullet that seemingly appeared from nowhere *inside* Kennedy's head – how?

Because of all the conspiracy theories flying around, the American government set up the Warren Omission to see if there were any omissions in the accepted assassination story. The Ommision decided that Oswald was a lonely assassin, which was compassionate, but no comfort to Jackie O'Kennedy. But that was the end of it. Case closed. Or was this still all part of a cover-up that went to the top, the *very* top?

THE MOON LANDINGS

Kennedy's dying wish was that man would one day talk on the moon. It was madness, but in the sixties America spent billions of dollars trying to send white men on a day trip to the moon in his memory. And by 16 July 1969 they felt

---

* Actually, this is my mate Paul's theory on what happened that day. He has seen the film *Jayeffkay* over 190 times, and he thinks that the fact that neither Oliver Stone nor Kevin Costner look into Jackie shooting John is all part of a conspiracy that goes to the top, the very top. When I ask him what this means he just repeats 'The *very* top', with a strong emphasis on the 'very', which I have shown on the written page with the use of italic letters, but I will show in the audiobook simply by saying it how he says it. Then he puts his finger to his lips, opens another can of Strongbow Cloudy Apple and checks the football scores on his phone.

they had almost got everything more or less worked out for the trip, and thought – fuck it – let's just give it a shot, what's the worst that can happen? – and so launched Apollo Seven-Eleven.

The launch was a success, but the moon men quickly discovered facilities on the moon were limited: the landscape wasn't even in colour, and there wasn't much to do. So they stuck a flag in it, played a round of golf and flew home. But such was the conspiratorial nature of the times, that some doubted man had walked on the moon at all, and many suggested the whole thing was faked, that the footage had been filmed on Mars, painted to look like the moon.

The Sixties in the UK

America wasn't the only country to have a sixties; incredibly, Britain had one too. In sixties Britain, nobody wanted to be seen working for the Establishment or wearing a suit. Because Britain had a new hero: super-cool spy James Bond, who worked for the Establishment, and wore a suit.

THE BEATLES

You can't write about sixties Britain without talking about the Fab Four, the Teletubbies of their time: Ringo, George, and Jean-Paul – The Beatles. These four lads were from Liverpool, but instead of just moaning or hanging around the docks, they did something about it and ended up living somewhere nice, thanks to writing some of the songs that have ever been written.

Success came quickly. But The Beatles were ruined the moment they joined the army, under the orders of Sergeant Pepper. He put them in uniforms and made them grow moustaches like their dads. For the band who had once rebelled against Britain's old guard, it was all over. For their last concert, they couldn't even get a venue. They had to do it on a roof, like randy cats.

COOL BRITANNIA

But it wasn't just music that put Britain back on the map it had never actually been off; anything British was now cool, not just the weather.

The British car to be seen getting out of was the Mini, which was short for 'miniskirt', and the skirt to be seen getting out of it in was the miniskirt, named after the popular small car.

All British films were cool, even the ones pretending to be foreign, like *The Italian Job* and the Jack Clouseau movies and *Carry On Up The Khyber*.

Fittingly, Britain even had a cool Prime Minister. With his Gannex raincoat, love of statistics and constant pipe-smoking, Harold Wilson was the epitome of the hedonistic sixties.

America in the Seventies

WATERGATE

The conspiracy theories of sixties America became conspiracy actuallies in the 1970s with the Watergate scandal. It was a cover-up that went to the top, the *very* top.

The affair started when President Nick's son sent some plumbers to fix a water-gate. The President denied all knowledge of the event, but *Washington Post*men Wood Wood and Bernie Stein unravelled the conspiracy by doing deep throat with an informer in a car park, and he happily spilled his beans.

The *Washington Post*men revealed that the President had lied through his big teeth, and he was eventually forced to resign. He was immediately flown by helicopter to confess all to David Frost.

The Viet-Nam War

Nixon left just after he had won, or at least drawn, or at least not lost too badly, the Viet-Nam War, which had been going on for twenty years. The Asian country had been divided into two halves – Viet and Nam. Viet in the North was communist and led by Dr Ho. Nam, the South, was not communist and America wanted it to stay that way. The

United A of S was worried about the domino theory, which said that if the South fell to communism, then there'd be no chance of Dominos pizzas establishing a foothold in the region. Capitalism would have lost.

American involvement in Viet/Nam intensified after an incident at a golf course in Tonkin. Soon thousands of Americans were flying to Vietnam, lured by the balmy weather, unrivalled nightlife and friendly locals. They were fighting the Viet Kong, a local version of King Kong with the Kong spelt differently (like when you see a drink called Diet Cock in foreign countries) to avoid IP disputes with the estate of Edgar Wallace and RKO, which is the last thing the Kong needed since they were already in one dispute with the two-faced American Satan.

But this Viet Kong proved harder to beat than the King kind. This Kong never climbed up tall buildings to roll barrels at its enemies. Instead it did the opposite, digging tunnels and blending into the jungle. If that is the opposite of throwing barrels.

More troops were needed, with many young American men simply blown there when they failed to dodge a strong draft. It was a brutal, scathing war, even when cut to the chart-topping, toe-tapping sounds of the Rolling Stones, Creedence Clearwater Revival and Jim E. Hendrix. Eventually, the Americans gave up, said 'Good evening Vietnam!' and took off from a helicopter from the roof of the American Embassy, before the Kong could scale the building and pluck the aircraft from the sky.

Viet and Nam were reunited as Vietnam. America was humiliated. It never wanted to think about Vietnam again. Which is why it is the only subject of all American films made between 1978 and 2002.

The UK in the Seventies

Just as quickly as the swinging sixties arrived in Britain, they were over, in almost exactly ten years. Everything that was once colourful went brown. It was like summer turning to winter or a bag of salad going off in the fridge when you haven't even had any of it.

In the nineteenth century, Britain had been known as the worktop of the world; by the 1970s, other, more foreign countries turned out to be better at making and doing stuff than Britain. And now, unlike the sixties, it was embarrassing being British. Like it should be.

The 1970s was a decade of Irish Troubles and industrial strife. The price of stuff was going up faster than wages. People went on strike and demanded more money, but it didn't work. Turned out nobody wanted to pay workers to stand round a bin on fire. Because that wasn't their job. Especially if they were firemen, or binmen.

With so much industrial unrest, the economy faltered. Suddenly British people couldn't afford to buy many of the shiny new brown things on offer, like the Curly Wurly or the Austin Allegro. Annoyed that they couldn't afford a tiny chocolate ladder, or a car that looked like a headmaster's shoe, after a hard day underground, the miners went on strike.

It sounds like magic, but coal actually contains electricity – and with no new coal, electricity had to be rationed. This was the 'three-day week', but they could have called it the more desirable 'four-day weekend'. The electric kept going off. People had to watch their TV by candlelight, only to find it wasn't even on.

And it wasn't just ordinary people who had problems hanging on to power. The 1970s contained four different Prime Ministers, like 2022. Political turmoil, like ordinary extra-virgin turmoil, or a bin, can easily catch fire. Anti-establishment attitudes were on the rise: graffiti, self-sufficiency, the Krankies . . . and punk.

PUNK

Punk was a cultural shift in music and menswear. It was about anger. It was about change, it was about giving an unusual amount of airtime to noisy bog-eyed little men who appealed to people with swastika jewellery.

Punks liked wearing leather and plastic bondage gear, and thought the state should be smashed up. They were basically the Conservative Party but from crap schools. Except him from The Clash.

Punks looked amazing. They covered themselves with spikes and pins, like it was hedgehog cosplay. The most famous punks were The Sexy Pistols. In 1977, the year of the Queen's Silverwear Jubilee, Johnny Rotten and the other members of the band, Paul, Jones, George and Ringo, released a single so controversial that when it became the national anthem, they had to give it a different tune: 'God Save The Queen'.

The BBC banned 'God Save The Queen', which meant nobody could celebrate the Queen's Silver Jubilee, and a new national anthem had to be invented: 'Mull Of Kintyre' by The New Beatles. It topped the chart in 1977 and stayed there until the singer of The Beatles was shot, three years later, in one of the most tragic acts of music criticism ever.

EUROPE

Britain joined the European Common Market, which was thought to be the cure for all of Britain's problems. We'd be in the world's biggest trading blob and use European money to invest in our industry. And we would never go to war with Germany again. Apart from that last point, it was perfect. It solved everything. Everyone was very happy with the idea, and always would be.

Some people said that Britain would lose sovereignty, but for most people that wasn't a big deal, since no one had used sovereigns for ages, except to make rings for loud-mouth scaffolders.

America in the Eighties

After being humbled by Vietnam in the seventies, America decided to shake it off and look like it didn't care by having an eighties-themed party: the clothes, the music, the economic policies, they would all be perfectly eighties. Because it was the eighties and that was all that was available in the shops, stores and central banks.

The eighties began with the election of a new President played by Hollywood goofball Ronald Reagan. Reagan had a simple, warmed-hearted message for every American – Get Rich Or Fuck Off. Suddenly it was okay to be rich, and shy millionaires, previously afraid of negative reaction to their disgusting wealth, could at last reveal themselves in public in TV shows like *Dallas*. And all TV shows were like *Dallas*.

Reagan loved money. He said that 'greedy is goody' and 'lunch is for pimps'. He masterminded a new sort of economy where even those at the bottom could get rich. He called it a 'tickle/drown economy' – because either you were tickled by the ludicrousness of the idea, or you would drown yourself in despair.

The idea was that money would pass from the very rich to the poor, which was a new way of saying the money would probably just fall out of the rich people's pockets while they were reaching for some champagne, and the poor could pick it up off the floor a coin at a time, giving them back their self-respect.

New electronic trading meant that money could be moved instantly from place to place, instead of having to put it all in those little see-through bags and weigh it at the post office.

Alongside this invention, Reagan invented a new breed of noisy, stripy humans called the yuppy. Yuppies were sort of financial wasps, but instead of hanging around sandwiches, they hung around money, and buzzed not because they were beating their wings together, but because they were off their tits on gak.

The yuppies became rich because they had an early sort of smartphone called a Filofax. It told them the order that days came in and what they were doing when. They literally knew the future.

But the yuppies weren't just twats. They worked hard – at doing whatever it was they did – and played hard – at putting stuff up their noses. Which gave them the energy to play even harder. And be even bigger twats. Suddenly it was trendy to be a massive banker. Wall Street was Cool Street. In the seventies, Studio 54 was where the cocaine was at; by the eighties it was up a mortgage advisor's nose.

This new lust for money changed fashion. Women wore power suits with shoulder pads stuffed with money. While female role models were once scientists and activists like Marie Curie and Rosa Parks, now female role models were more likely to be Alexis Colby Carrington, Madonna making sparks come out of her bra or Alan Greenspan, chairman of the US Federal Reserve.

SPACE SHUTTLE

By the 1980s, the NASA[*] realised that people didn't believe man had been to the moon, no matter how many times

---

[*] New American Space Army

they pretended to go. So they stopped firing rockets upwards and then blowing them up so people would think they were on the moon, and swapped to rockets that came back to earth after a bit. These could be used to pretend to go into space multiple times, saving a lot of real money.

The Space Shuttle looked like a plane with an impulse-eating problem, and was launched by tying it to some rockets, like mental teenagers do with cats. It was first launched in 1981 and was such a good idea that they stopped doing it forever in 2011.

The shuttle was covered in ceramic tiles, like your mum's kitchen, and got incredibly hot on re-entry, like your mum. If any of the tiles fell off, which they often did, the shuttle would have overheated and exploded on the way back from space, a nail-biting situation for ground control which one famous mission avoided by blowing up before it could get to the crucial point of danger.

Because they weren't sure it would work, the first Space Shuttle wasn't bought by NASA, but hired from car-rental firm Enterprise, with their logo prominently displayed on the nose bit. This successful product placement led to the full fleet of Space Shuttles being sponsored by Atlantic (the airline), Challenge and Discovery (the TV channels), and celebrity detectives Columbo and Endeavour.

When the Space Shuttle was in space, it could put boring satellites into orbit, do experiments children asked for (usually growing cress in an egg), and sometimes a man would go out on a stick and then come back in. The Space Shuttle never had a battle or landed anywhere, or fought aliens. It was by any standard the worst spaceship ever made.

To date, the Space Shuttle is the only American space vehicle in which James Bond has sexed up a floating woman while some old men watched.

Britain in the Eighties

In 1978, literally everyone in Britain went on strike, which led to corpses being piled up in Leicester Square as people died waiting for the striking cinemas to open. Rubbish went unburied. So it was a dirty and smelly time, and it became known as the Winter of Malcontent.

This led to the election of a new, and quite markable Prime-Numbered minister in 1979. Margaret 'Mrs' Thatcher – the i-Ron Lady – the face of Britain in the eighties. With her love of monetarism, supply-side economics and fiscal conservatism, Thatcher was very much a man of the people.

Thatcher's original name was Margaret Roberts, but she changed it to Mrs Thatcher to show how much she loved a dangerous new ideology: Thatcherism.

Thatcher got into power by making her squeaky woman's voice go much lower like a man. This made it easier to take her seriously, even though she still carried a woman's handbag. If you closed your eyes, it was like being bossed about in the dark by a husky schoolboy, which a lot of the privately educated members of the Conservative Party could relate to.

After her election, standing on the steps of 10 Down Street – the only address in London named after a crossword clue – Mrs Thatcher promised to bring 'harmony, truth and faith', starting a tradition of lying on pavements that Prime Ministers continue to this day.

Thatcher promised economic freedom, which meant anyone could get rich. Provided they already had loads of spare money and didn't need to be rich. It's a system we have in place to this day.

Politicians in the olden days often tried to help the poor, who usually turned out to be ungrateful, so Mrs Thatcher had a new plan. She would help the poor by helping the rich, who were nicer to hang around with. Mrs Thatcher invented something called Reaganomics, which meant that if you helped the rich, the poor would look after themselves. And if they didn't, you couldn't see them anyway because the rich were in the way, and their houses were enormous.

THE ROYAL WEEDING

One thing the Prime Mrs-ter Thatcher hadn't sold off was the royal family, because they were on the banknotes, which would have made the deal confusing. And it was lucky she didn't, because the country was about to party like it was 1981. Which it was. In July 1981, the futuristic king of England, then plain Prince of Charles, married the then effervescent Lady Di.

It was a fairytale wedding, with magic and castles and a

beautiful princess and maybe even a pea. Though if there had been a pea, Diana probably wouldn't have eaten it, because of the hideous pressure she was under to be thin.

LADY DI

Lady Diana Spencer was dubbed 'Shy Di' because of her unrivalled prowess at the coconut shy, something that attracted the attention of young, coconut-obsessive Prince Charles.

THE FORKLANDS

There was only one thing that would bring the country together more than a fairytale wedding, and that was a fairytale war.

In 1982, a British island called Forklands Island was stolen. Britain didn't want anyone to steal their Forklands Island, which is why they'd put it safely 8,000 miles away. What Britain didn't realise is that 8,000 miles away was exactly where a country called Argentinia was hiding, hidden behind the equator. And when no one was looking, the Argies invaded.

Mrs Thatcher was furious. An amazing thing happened. Before her Cabinet's astonished eyes, she turned into an Iron Lady. No footage of this transformation exists, but the exciting Hollywood blockbuster *Iron Man* might give us some idea. Mrs Thatcher would have had all bits of metal whoosh onto her legs and arms in an amazing suit-up sequence. She would have flown thrillingly through the sky on rocket shoes. And she would have wisecracked inside a helmet.

The Argentinians couldn't fight an Iron Lady. They were simple people, armed with only sticks and grass. Like Ewoks. The war was over quickly. Soon, above Forklands Island, there was something red, white and blue. Not a tomato, a ghost and a Smurf, but the flag that makes any British heart proud: the Onion Jack.

Like all wars, this war made every single person in the country happy. Britain had won back a piece of land as vital to the national identity as the old Wembley Stadium, The Crooked House pub or that humble cornfield where the Battle of Britain was won in 1066 by King Harold Churchill.

THE MOANERS' STRIKE

Having retaken Forklands Island, Mrs Thatcher swept back into power at the 1983 election. Now that everyone knew her superhero secret identity she was more popular than ever. She was so popular, she started to do unpopular things, just for the sheer hell of it.

In 1984 she started another war, this time with the miners. The miners had always annoyed Mrs Thatcher because they liked to get together and ask to be paid properly, and when that catches on, the whole country gets really expensive and you need to make a cheaper one.

Mrs Thatcher decided the miners needed to be taught a lesson. It would be her defining moment. Normally if you want to deal with something that lives underground that's annoying you, you flatten the hills and put down traps. But Mrs Thatcher decided to use the police.

Mrs Thatcher's enemy was King Arthur Scargill, who looked like a seagull poking its head through a Shredded Wheat. The Iron Lady eventually beat her arch nemesis, and made powerful unions something only a lunatic would think of bringing back, like child labour, or Thatcherism.

It was one of the most bitterest industrial disputes in British history – but without it, we wouldn't have the film *Pride*, which is quite good. Solid three stars. So we ought to thank the miners, and the policemen who were paid to beat the miners up.

Whole bits of the country never recovered from the strike. Surrey and Berkshire for instance, became places where thousands of red-faced middle-aged men could only achieve erections while imagining Mrs Thatcher ordering a baton charge.

THATCHER OUT

The eighties ended in 1990 with the series finale of Mrs Thatcher. She had spent eleven years at Number Ten, a record that would remain unbroken until the following year, when Bryan Adams beat her by spending sixteen weeks at number one.

Thatcher was destroyed by her own party, as certainly as Michael Barrymore was, after she refused to back down on a new tax called the pole tax which she'd come up with. This new tax was the most unpopular tax since they taxed windows in the 18,000th century, forcing ordinary people to switch to Apple Macs. People could do without windows, but Britain needs poles. Without poles, you can't fly flags. You can't do a decathlon. You can't support a marquee for a cake-judging competition. If you tax poles, you tax *Britain*. This time Thatcher had gone too far – and she was sent packing.

When Mrs Thatcher left Number Ten, she even cried some tears, which she had never done before, in case she rusted. The Iron Lady was no more. But Thatcherism wasn't the only ism on the way out . . .

The End of Communism

The end of communism had started when the Russians got a new leader: Michael Gorbachev. He launched two new policies: *Glasnost*, which means Glasnost, and *Perestroika*, which doesn't. These policies gave the people of Eastern Europe a taste of freedom. And it tasted exactly as they expected: of Big Mac and Lynx Africa.

The Iron Curtain was opened in 1989 to give the people of the East a chance to see how lucky they were not to have to live the life of a decadent Western imperialist. But in fact the very opposite happened. They decided they liked the life of a decadent Western imperialist and they weren't going back. Even the worst excesses of Western capitalism – demonstrated by the music of David Hasselhoff – could not put off the Eastern Europeans. Every country wanted to be Western. The Cold War was over. Over forty years it never really got hot, like the shower in a Travelodge.

> **IMMERSIVE HISTORY: THE COLD WAR**
>
> 1. Build a Berlin Wall in your garden. Get the neighbours to dress as border guards and tell them to shoot on sight.
> 2. Throw a Chinese Communist Party. Ask permission.
> 3. Look into the abyss of nuclear armageddon.
> 4. You are President Ronald Reagan. What are you thinking about?
> 5. Do a light aerobic workout to the sound of Phil Collins' 'Sus-sus-udio'. Feel the burn.

America in the Nineties

With a mathematical predictability that borders on laziness, America followed the eighties with the so-called nineties. The nineties was pretty similar to the eighties except that, with the Cold War over, everyone could really concentrate on just having a good time without the fear of nuclear armageddon putting a crimp in their day.

The figurehead of this permanent party atmosphere was sexy saxophonist and President Billiam Clinton. If anything, Clinton had a little too much fun. Like Nixon before him, Clinton was brought down by a leak: his penis leaked onto bubbly intern Monica Lewinsky's dress, she never got round to dry-cleaning it (because, like me, she knows dry-cleaning is a rip-off) and he was almost impeached as a result.

Because it revolved around Clinton's wonky penis, rather

than Nixon's systematic undermining of the US justice system, this was thought of as the more humorous of the two presidential impeachments of the late twentieth century, and as traumatic as it was for him at the time, I'm sure he has a cheeky chuckle about it now.

THE INTERNET

Clinton's impeachment was *so* funny that people wanted to read about it as soon as possible, so they had to use computers to spread the gory details. Because it was about Clinton's affair with an intern they called this computer network the intern-net. Rumours about Clinton's infidelity could now fly across the planet at the speed of binary, because all the big computers in the world had been linked up.

The computers had been linked up for a while, by Tim, Berners and Lee, but until now, there was nothing good to read on them – just GeoCities and a boiling kettle in a lab somewhere. Clinton's shenanigans changed all that; it was the first killer app and the start of the WWW: World War Web. In time, the internet would even change the way we think, making it harder to do than ever before.

The Wide World Wide Web Wide was, in many ways, very much the internet of its day, and we still use the term now, though instead of the three-syllable name 'world wide web', we abbreviate it to the nine-syllable 'www'.

Before the www, if you wanted to know something that wasn't true, you had to go to a library, and not read a book properly. Now that can be done in half the time, walking down the street not looking where you're going.

The Nineties in the UK

If the 1980s in the UK were all about money, which they were, then the 1990s were all about fun, which they were. In the eighties there were only two colours – red and chrome – but in the 1990s there were millions of colours, at least 256 – everything was bright and garish, like everyone was a Muppet. Even Chris Evans looked normal. This was the decade of art, music, Tinky Winky, Dipsy, Laa-Laa and Jamie Oliver.

NEW LABOUR

Even politics got a dose of fun. After Mrs Thatcher, there had been a sort of grey hospital administrator called Major John in charge for a bit, and politics badly needed some oomph. Britain was taken over, in a putsch called 'coup Britannia', by an advertising salesman called Tony Blair. He dragged Britain into the twentieth century, just in time for the twenty-first century.

Blair revitalised the Labour Party. He even renamed it 'New Labour' so it wouldn't be confused with the old one full of Tony Benn and pork pies and British Rail and smells. With his youthful looks and electric guitar, Tony Blair was very of his time. And on 2 May 1997, Tony Blair triumphantly entered Down Street on a landslide, though not an actual landslide like they have in the Dolomites, which meant the death toll was lower.

COOL BRITS

To celebrate his victory, Blair hosted a party at Number Ten.

The event was dubbed the Cool Britannia party, but how cool can a party be where you have to put your glasses on coasters and you might end up chatting to Robin Cook? It was a who's who of 'who's that prick?' Jarvis Cooker, Damon Altern-8, Noelandliam Gallagher – none of the actually cool people went. Instead there was Mick Hucknall and Baldrick.

It was the start of Blair's post-pop career as a living saint. Through the nineties he solved all the nation's problems – the economy, health, education, education, education, even the Irish Troubles – there was nothing he couldn't do. Except tell the truth. But soon there were no problems left in Britain for Blair to solve, so he had to start solving problems in other countries. Even if they didn't want him to.

The Rest of the World 1945–2000

History also took place in other countries in the world during this period, for example, New Zealand.

Chapter Ten
The Global Globe

2000–NOW

As we entered the twenty-first century, we were faced with horror after horror. Bird flu. 9/11. The invasion of Iraq. The financial crash. And the Jonas Brothers.

But it wasn't all horror: the twenty-first century has also been marked by incredible technological advances that would baffle our grandfathers, let alone a nomadic herdsman in twelfth-century Albania, or me.

Phones got smaller, and then got bigger again. And then became watches. New technology means you're as likely to be reading this on an iPad or robot dog's eyeball as you are in a book.

All the previous chapters should really be considered as build-up to this ultimate finale. Until now I've been looking at history that most people were dead for. In this chapter I'll be looking at history that people have lived through. So I'm going to have to check my facts for a change. Or someone is. I hope it's someone else because in anticipation of finishing this book soon, I've booked two weeks on the popular Greek island Mykonos on lastminute.com, a website that is now also part of history.

This chapter recalls history so fresh that it's almost not history and just some recent events. And then towards the end of the book, it won't even be history at all, just the news.

This is the end of history books. They will never need to write a history book again. At least not quite like this one.

....

THE COMPUTER

A surprisingly short time ago, the word 'computer' wouldn't have meant much at all, and it's only really in the last thirty years that they've crept quietly and inexorably into our lives, like K-pop and chlamydia.

Globalisation

By the start of the twenty-first century, with communism long dead, capitalism had triumphed. Now everyone in the world was free to make money, as long as they had some in the first place.

Suddenly everyone was making money on stocks and shares and derivatives and ISAs and Leeds Building Society Liquid Gold accounts. Everyone – apart from poor people – was making so much money that there wasn't room to store it all in cash. So it had to be stored safely behind computer screens. Storing your money on a computer was safe, as long as you could remember your PIN code and your mother's maiden name, and could afford a computer.

And now, with all computers linked together by the internet, people could now trade with anyone all over the world – something called globalisation. The world was becoming dominated by huge global corporations like the nice one publishing this book – my favourite global corporation – and other less good ones.

But what even is a computer? I haven't mentioned it before because it's quite complicated to explain and I thought I could get away without mentioning it, but I still have 5,000 words to write before I can get on that plane to Mykonos so I'm going to have to do it in quite a lot of mind-numbing detail now.

THE STORY OF COMPUTERS

Today, computers are everywhere. They're on our desks, in our pockets; they're even in our fridges if you have a smart fridge or you've put your laptop in the salad drawer. We wear computers, interact with them and let them run our lives, all without sparing them a microsecond's thought as they plot together to take over the planet.

But, as anyone over the age of forty-six knows, it wasn't always this way.

So how did we get here? And what is a computer anyway? Could we eventually be replaced by computers? And will I be asking more rhetorical questions as I go along? To fill up my word count? Are you about to find out? The answer to all these questions is: yes.

WHAT ARE COMPUTERS?

Computers are basically machines for doing fast sums. Like, if you're trying to add up while being chased by a shark, you need a computer. Computers run on maths. Or math if you're reading this in America. Computers, basically, make maths disappear. And that's good news for me, because maths is one of three things I can't stand. Four things I can't stand.

WHEN WAS THE FIRST COMPUTER?

The first computer was invented by a man called Charles 'Cabbage' Babbage and programmed by a woman called Ada Lovelace in eighteen something. Ada Lovelace was a pioneering woman who helped create the computing technology that today allows women to have dick pics sent to them. It seems strange today, but Ada Lovelace was her real name, not her dating profile handle.

Sadly Babbage and Lovelace's computer arrived before there were any good games for it, and it never took off. Like the Oric, which was only big in France, where they use computers for philosophy, not playing rip-offs of *Galaxian*.

ALAN TURING

Alan Turing, who despite his name never actually went on tour, is now recognised by many as the 'Father of Modern Computing', but recognised by more as Benedict Cumberbatch. Alan Turing's vision was a revolutionary one, and it helped shape computing as we know it today, at least as much as Steve Jobs or *Super Mario* did.

During the war, to crack German codes and help Britain stay free of the Nazis, Alan Turing built the Colossus computer at top Allied theme park Bletchley Park, surrounded by predominantly female code breakers. He must have loved having all those pretty young women around him.

Actually no, because, in an amazing twist typical of Benedict Cumberbatch's work, Turing was gay. And so after he'd cracked the Nazi codes and saved the universe, he got his reward: being chemically castrated by a grateful nation until he committed suicide.

MODERN COMPUTERS

The Electronic Numerical Integrator and Computer at the University of Pennsylvania was the next first computer. Constructed in June 1945 it was built just months too late to challenge Hitler to a game of Pong on. With their huge tape machines and flashing lights, old computers look funny to us now. Like something from an old film. Or an Adam Curtis documentary.

The first computers were so big that they had to be kept locked up in huge rooms in case they turned against their human enslavers and went on a rampage, but luckily computers keep getting smaller, and are now easier to tame.

Even now we have laptops, which is like a computer but smaller and simpler to steal. It's amazing to think that even crime can benefit from technology.

WHAT'S THE FUTURE FOR COMPUTERS?

It's ironic for me to say that the words you're reading now were written on a computer. But one day a computer might have written them all by itself. And then a computer might read them. And where does that leave us humans? Dying from lung poisoning in the silicon mines? Makes you think. But not as fast as a computer can. Or maybe at all. Perhaps the computers have won already?

Climate Change

In the twenty-first century, even to people constantly staring at the I Can Has Cheezburger website on their computer screen, a grave fact was now clear to everyone: the earth was dying. The seas swallowing land. Great fires raging across the planet. It sounds like the plot from a science fiction novel. But it wasn't. It was happening. It's called climate change, and it might seem new and scary, but it started ages ago, like *Doctor Who*.

What is climates? Climates are temperatures that different countries have. They're why we go on holiday. Britain has a cold climate. Greece has a hot climate. Though it is more expensive than it used to be. But all that is set to change. If climate scientists are right, Britain will soon have a hot climate. And Greece will have melted – though will still be quite expensive.

Climate change was once called global warming, but they changed the name because people quite liked the idea of being warm and so carried on as usual. You get used to what climate you're in. If you're from Scotland, then Wales can feel hot. It isn't though. It's pretty miserable. But they're used to it there, because they never take their anoraks off.

Global warming is caused by the greenhouse effect, which is the cause of global warming. It's a vicious oblong. So what causes greenhouse gases? Well, we do, by burning fuels like coal and oil to make electricity. If you're reading this on an iPad, on a plane, licking batteries, you're contributing to global warming. So stop it! (Except reading or being on the plane.)

Greenhouse gases are making the North Pole melt, meaning too much sea. Not everyone wants to live in the sea. You don't need to be a scientist to know that; you just need to have seen *The Little Mermaid*. She hated it.

Sea levels have risen around 17 cm in the last one hundred years. Which means that when you go swimming it's even deeper and more dangerous. The sea levels are rising because the ice caps are melting. But it's not all bad news – less ice means less disasters like *Titanic*.

One of the reasons it's hard to work out what's going on is that not all scientists agree about climate change. Some scientists, like Nigel Farage, say fossil dinosaur fuels are the only way to power the economy, so we should use them all up as quickly as possible. We don't have dinosaurs any more, so why should we save the fuel they run on?

Some people say, well if this is global warming then bring it on – I don't mind a bit of nice weather. Ha ha ha ha ha ha – but I don't think you'll be laughing when your balls

THE GLOBAL GLOBE

are melting in unbearable heat, mate. If that's what happens.

But both sides of the debate agree we need to do something about it, and soon. Whether that something is something, or nothing.

One way of stopping the impact of global warming is to use carbon capture and storage. But it's complicated. Very complicated. So much so that I'm not even going to begin explaining how it works. Ask a friend, if they're a climate-change scientist who specialises in carbon capture. If you don't have any friends who are climate-change scientists, you're probably Donald Trump and don't give a shit, so it all works out.

Climate change means rethinking everything we do, even if we're not thinking in the first place, like me, right now, because I'm too hot. I might take this jumper off. That's better. Right. Where was I? Rethinking everything.

For example, at the moment I'm wearing three layers, including my unmentionables. And I'm feeling quite comfortable now. But it could be that in the future, I'll only need two. That's the prospect we're all going to have to face. And less layers means less fashion.

Smart.

Global Financial Crash

The whole globalisation thing was going well until 2008, when there was a huge global financial crisis. All the rich countries of the world pulled together to solve this crisis, in a way they've decided not to do about the global climate crisis. Because the global elite don't care about rising temperatures, but do care about falling stock prices.

The cause of the crash? Cheap mortgages in the 2000s had inflated a housing bubble in the US, and when it burst, Wall Street's famous Lemon Brothers collapsed in the shockwave; it was a sad day when the brothers' remains were taken out of the offices in small cardboard boxes by tearful former employees.

Bank after bank began to fail, each one putting pressure on the next; it was like a long line of dominoes, except with no cool bit where the falling dominoes make a pixel-like picture of Heather Locklear, and with substantially more quantitative easing.

Britain 2000–2020

GORGON BROWN

In 2007, Tony Blair sloped off, leaving Number Ten under the stewardship of his ghostly butler, Gorgon Brown. Blair had been fun. He was cool and good-looking. But he was crazy. And a warmonger. And a liar. He was like the fun boyfriend that you have at university but could never marry. Because he married someone else. Britain wanted to settle down with someone fiscally stable, prudent and dour: Gorgon Brown.

Ten years earlier leadership rivals Tony Blair and Gorgon Brown had carved out a historic deal in a fashionable London restaurant: Blair would put in seven quid because he hadn't had a starter and he had a coupon. But now it was Brown's turn to take his side of the bargain, and become PM.

THE BREXIT

But Brown didn't last long because he was so serious and committed and diligent, which to most Brits equals boring. So Britain got a new Prime Minister: 1930s waxwork cad David Cameron.

David Cameron decided to do something called a referendum to make Britain a more peaceful, united, strong and stable place. In an election politicians can say anything they like, and then not do it when they win, because it turns out it's really complicated. But in a referendum, you ignore that it's really complicated and just do it anyway, because it's not your fault. It's theirs. And that's democracy.

The referendum happened because some people in Britain felt restricted by being tied to Europe. There were fears about immigration and red tape and sovereignty and being made to eat foreign couscous instead of traditional British couscous.

One man, Nigel Fabergé, spoke louder than anyone else, although he wasn't an MP thanks to a sinister conspiracy of ordinary voters that had kept him out of Westminster. He'd spent so much time campaigning to leave the EU that he hadn't had a chance to work out what might actually happen if we did it.

On the Remain side, David Cameron went round the country doing what he did best, being pink and patronising, and giving people the good news about remaining. Most of the public paid no attention to the details of the referendum, and just relied on big words and big numbers, and a picture of foreigners queuing. It was the politics of fear. A simple message that chilled the nation's blood: if foreigners could queue, what did being British even mean?

The sun rose on 24 June 2016, and with it came the news that Britain had voted to leave the EU. For so long the parrot on Europe's shoulder, we were finally ready to fall off. That day, Britain had Brexit for breakfast. And would be eating a lot more Brexit every day for a good few years.

It was one of the biggest moments since moments were first invented. Britain had decided that it had become lost and needed to find itself again. And even if the answer to that question was obviously 'a bit up from France and to the left', maybe that wasn't a good-enough answer any more. Who wants to be given directions using France? What do they know about directions? They don't even drive on the correct side of the road.

If Britain was out of Europe, where should it go next? America? Maybe it could get closer to the Commonwealth. Maybe somewhere sunny like Gibraltar. But what if we don't like the food? And what if they don't have Bovril?

Still, a sense of national pride and disgust swept through the nation. Britain might have had internal disagreements but now everyone was all going to pull together and make Brexit work. Even if it could never work. And anyone who said otherwise was a saboteur, a Bremoaner or a so-called expert.

Britain had come a long way over millions of years without ever moving, and now for the first time it was leaving the place – Europe – it had called home for so long. That's if it can get the correct travel documents.

MAY

The Brexit result sent shockwaves through the political establishment. David Cameron resigned, and the new Prime Minister was Tresemmé, the posh French shampoo.

Even people that previously said that Brexit was a terrible idea, like the new PM, now said it was a fantastic idea, and she desperately tried to find a way of making it work in a way that meant Britain wasn't plunged back into the Dark Ages.

It was a time of great national pride. Everyone was proud to be British. Even if they were checking to see if they were maybe a little bit Irish so they could get a passport.

Coronavirus

Brexit meant that Britons had lost freedom of movement, but germs were free to travel anywhere in the world, without a passport. And that's what happened in 2020: coronavirus.

OUTBREAK

The virus first came to public attention on New Year's Eve 2019 when Chinese authorities announced that twenty-seven people in the city of Wuhan had caught an unexplained viral illness; but the world was too busy looking at fireworks explode over Sydney Harbour, and hoping its ex would text, to notice.

The source of the outbreak was traced to a so-called 'wet' market in the city; a wet market is a bit like a farmers' market, but with less locally sourced cheese, and a significantly larger proportion of live, diseased bats for sale.

THE SPREAD

By late January 2020 there were the first signs of the virus outside Wuhan, with cases in Beijing, Italy and Japan; perhaps spread there by travellers, or what makes more sense to me, bats. Because they can fly. And they were probably monked off that we were eating them. So this was the bats' payback.

By early February 2020 cases of the virus had been confirmed in Cambodia, Thailand and the Philippines, putting a real dent in the travel itineraries of European sex tourists, the forgotten victims of the disease.

Despite the threat, Europe carried on as usual: three thousand Atletico Madrid fans attended their side's Champions League game against Liverpool at Anfield stadium, despite Spain's increasing number of Covid cases. The game ended Liverpool 2 – Coronavirus 590.

We were beginning to learn what coronavirus looked like, so if you spotted it you could wash it off quickly. Coronavirus – part of a hardened gang known as The Covid Ne-ne-ne-ne-nineteen – was too powerful for normal flu remedies, even Night Nurse Day & Night, and that contains caffeine.*

LOCKDOWN

The UK government advised washing your hands a lot, as they tried to wash theirs of any blame for not being prepared for the pandemic. The message was a success: people were washing their hands more furiously than a businessman after a pre-meeting wank. The public started panic buying. At first it was toilet roll. Then big bags of pasta. Soon the shelves were empty and shoppers left with nothing in their hands. Except coronavirus.

Supermarkets had a new offer on: Panic Buy One Get One. There was so much panic-buying that at one stage Sainsbury's ran out of Nectar Points.

---

* I once took a Day Nurse pill in the night by mistake and I was awake till 5 a.m. with the lyrics to Black Lace's 'Superman' running through my head at double speed.

A shopping trip became frightening. Covid meant that you didn't need to skydive or ski to get your adrenaline running: you could be a thrill-seeker just by going to Lidl to get some Spicy Nik Naks. Well, the Lidl version of them.

People took a deep breath before going into the shop, which only made things worse. Toilet rolls were soon changing hands for huge sums – new or used. Copies of the new cash-in magazine *Panic Buyer Weekly* were flying off the shelves.

The government also advised social distancing – which was like when you cancel someone on the internet, except you were cancelling them in real life, and it wasn't just that bloke with a Union Jack as his avatar: it was everyone who lives on the entire planet. The government said people shouldn't get closer than two metres, but, after Brexit, no one knew how long two metres was, and so they died, the so-called metric martyrs. If you give the other person a tape measure to hold to measure it, they might give it back to you with coronavirus on it. Not deliberately.

Social distancing was a really good excuse for not seeing people that you don't want to see anyway. You had to remember not to touch your face. But how would blind people know who they were in the morning?

It turned out the people we need to keep the country running in a crisis – nurses, supermarket workers and street cleaners – are not very well paid. And the people we don't need at all are the people who get paid the most

– footballers, talking-heads people on TV and Richard Branson. It's like there was something wrong at the very heart of society. People promised this would change, but then forgot about it later in the euphoria of being able to leave the house for an hour a day.

The rising death toll took a toll on life. The streets were full of people in masks. It was like we were all going to a fancy-dress party as worried anaesthetists. The UK Government put the entire population in lockdown: you were allowed to go out only for one of four reasons: exercise, shopping, medical emergency, and to take pictures of people breaking the rules.

You weren't allowed to see anyone and had to spend all day in your room. It was a bit like being a goth. Gatherings of more than two in a park were made illegal. Which really decimated the dogging industry, something that Britain led the world in.

It was very easy for intellectuals like me to go into lockdown because I just did what I normally do – watch some YouTube clips about hair-straighteners and leaf through the *Sunday Times Style* magazine, once I'd swabbed it down with some Jeyes Fluid.

Work changed: people were suddenly having online Zoom teleconference meetings and it really made you think 'Why did anyone bother going to the office in the first place?' People were having Zoom dinner parties, Zoom pub quizzes, Zoom games nights – it was awful. Suddenly people who you would try never to meet in real life were getting in touch – and you had no excuse not to see them. Except that your broadband had gone wonky.

Personally I was all right in lockdown but I think my friend Paul lost it. He quarantined himself in his flat and never came out and I left him a cheese sandwich outside his door every night. One morning it was still there and I thought he was a goner but it turned out he'd just fallen asleep binge-watching *Tiger King*.

Even Prime Minister Boris Johnson caught the 'catching the bug' bug and he wound up in intensive care. Which must have been a real eye-opener for him, because he had never seemed to intensively care about anything or anyone before.

In the US, armed protestors demanded an end to the lockdown. Schools and malls must reopen, they argued, to give a boost to America's lone-shooter industry. Guns were useless against the virus, which it turns out is much smaller than is shown in the pictures.

President Donald Trump initially said that the virus was no more dangerous than influenza and the pandemic was a hoax, dismissing coronavirus as 'Fake Flus'. Trump suggested injecting bleach to combat the virus. Doctors say you shouldn't use bleach internally, but some people do bleach their bumhole – does that count as internal or external? It's sort of east meets west – fusion flesh; the bumhole is the Istanbul of the body.

THE GLOBAL GLOBE

REPERCUSSIONS

The world's finances took a battering. Some economists worried that without a functioning world economy there would be huge unemployment, especially among economists. They believed there was a clear danger that, until we found a cure, capitalism wouldn't be able to fully destroy the planet.

CORONAVIRUS

Not actual size. Or it would have been easier to catch, and we wouldn't have had to wash our shopping.

Twenty-First-Century American Presidents

GEORGE W. BUSH

George W. Bush was the second George W. Bush to be president, except the first one had an H between the George and the W. If this sounds like too much of a coincidence to be true, I couldn't give a shit and nor could America.

He'd only been president for a few months when a bunch of trainee pilots failed their flying exams by driving some planes into floors 9 to 11 of the World Trade Center. They were from Afghanistan, controlled by a man on a horse called Osama bin Laden, so George Bush invaded Iraq, because it was only a couple of countries away and the bloke who ran it had tried to kill his dad (the George with the H).

This was called The War On Terror, and in 2003 Bush declared it was over. It went on for another twenty years. He didn't. In 2008 he retired to his farm to do the sort of paintings you put on fridges.

BARACK OBAMA

Barack Obama was the next President, and everyone thought he was amazing. But Barack Obama was nice only up to a limit. He tracked down bin Laden to an Airbnb in Pakistan. He sent in the Naval Seals to kill him and such was the violence of their mission that it is doubtful bin Laden got his

Airbnb deposit back. Indeed, he may have had to pay an additional cleaning charge. My sources tell me that, even today, the inventory is incomplete and the Airbnb host is demanding payment for a missing lemon squeezer, and for the removal of a damaged UH-60 Black Hawk helicopter from the yard.

He was happy, and so was America. The USA was having its best life, and it almost seemed too good to be true. And sure enough . . .

OH FUCKING HELL IT'S DONALD TRUMP

With Barack Obama being so popular, everybody thought that racism had gone away in America. But racism bravely fought back in the shape of Donald Trump.

Trump had been on TV for years as a horrible boss, so he was the perfect man for the job of being back on TV being a horrible boss, but this time to the whole country, not just some game-show contestants who couldn't run a lemonade stand properly. To a lot of people he was a breath of fresh air, saying the things that 'no-one else would say', but which those people actually said all the time.

Then in 2020 there was an election, and Trump said he won it, even though he didn't. And finally his supporters lost their shit with him and invaded the Capitol (which is their Hogwarts) and tried to hang Mike Pence, who was the VicePonald, to show how disappointed they were in him. And everyone thought that would be it for Trump. They were wrong.

JOE BIDEN

Joe Biden was basically Father Christmas but without the beard, the red suit, the reindeer, the elves, the presents, the grottos or the ho-ho-ho-ing.

I would say more, but there's a pizza just arrived, and I think he may be on the way out the White House anyway.

Britain 2019–2024ish

BORIS JOHNSON

Boris Johnson became Prime Minister in July 2019 and he turned out to be an unorthodox Prime Minister. When he couldn't get his Brexit deal through Parliament, he switched the whole building off and back on again. Some members of the judging community told him this was illegal, so he decided to have a Snap Election just before Christmas, so everyone was already cold and busy and knackered and running out of money. Johnson won, beating a solid candidate in Jeremy Corbyn, a wooden mannequin from a museum display about the golden age of men standing round burning bins.

Then 2020 came along, promising great things for Great Britain. Johnson said this was the year he'd 'get Brexit done', by which he meant he'd stop saying 'Get Brexit Done'. And he did! Although mainly because, with Covid knocking the breath out of everyone, he had to replace it with his new slogan, 'Stay Home, Protect The NHS, Save Lives' and its disappointing sequels, 'Stay Alert, Control The Virus, Save Lives' and 'Try To Stay At Home But Go To School And Dine Out To Help Us Out'.

Turns out, while he was getting us to stay at home and not see each other, he and some work-experience people called Ben and Shaun and Ben and Minty and Bunty and Jonty and Ben were having piss-ups at Number Ten. Johnson said no piss-ups had happened. Then he said he didn't know about the piss-ups that didn't happen. Then he asked someone to look into the piss-ups that didn't happen. Some members of the policing community told him this was illegal, so he admitted to Parliament that he was sorry but that he didn't know about the piss-ups he was at that didn't happen.

Finally, some members of the Just Shut Up And Tell Us The Truth community hauled him up in front of their committee, and said that all this bullshit was enough to get him kicked out of office. But Johnson beat them at their own game, resigning from the job and proving he hadn't told any lies at all, otherwise he'd have been kicked out of office.

LIZ TRUSS

What happened next was just plain weird.

There was this woman called Liz Truss, who nobody really knew much about, but she was famous for talking about the disgrace of cheese and the potential of pork. Bit niche, but, you know. She was only in charge for about thirty minutes but in that time she killed two things: the

British Economy, and Her Majesty The Queen Elizabeth The Second Of The Eighth Of September.

She was stopped before she could kill again.

RICHY SUNAK

The next Prime Minister No One Voted For was 'Richy' Sunak, who was so-called because he had made millions and demonstrated great financial nouse by marrying wisely. He was a sort of tetchy action figure who looked all shiny and couldn't stop grinning sympathetically whenever anyone told him they were having a hard time or couldn't get a break or a hospital appointment or a job or their heads around why he was Prime Minister.

He is still PM as I write, incredibly. But I doubt he will be by publication.*

Culture Wars

After the two world wars, the planet was at total peace for many decades, not counting all the other wars that there were all over the planet all the time. It was truly a time of previously unknown harmony and peace (in certain limited

---

* Just as this book was going to press, President Sunak daringly and stupidly called an election that he knew he couldn't win, but wanted to have before the school holidays kicked in. My publisher told me there was still time to include a section on his successor, but I pretended I didn't have very good reception because I was already on my way to Stansted.

areas, subject to availability). But soon that fragile peace (see conditions, please ask your server) would be shattered by a new war: a culture war, between the woke and the anti-woke.

'Woke' was a new word for the awful people who thought about other people and whether you might be hurting their feelings. These dreadful humans would guess whether you might annoy someone who wasn't there, and then tell you off for upsetting someone they'd imagined. And that made you feel terrible. So now there was definitely someone with hurt feelings, and it was you. Which is apparently better.

To lots of 'anti-woke' people this idea of 'woke' seemed mental, but they now weren't allowed to call it that any more, in case mental people complained. The only thing in favour of 'woke' was that these 'anti-woke' people were the absolutely very worst people in the world.

These culture wars meant that nobody can talk to their dad or their nan any more, and that may eventually lead to one of the longest periods of peace on earth.

SMARTPHONES

Woke v. anti-woke polarisation was fuelled by the invention of the smartphone.

In 2007 Steve Jobs, who was a sort of middle-aged Harry Potter but with none of the friends, launched the first smart phone: the Apple iPhone 3. More than anything in history, this was the single device that revolutionised going to the toilet.

The smartphone is little bigger than a chocolate bar, twice as addictive as one, and like a chocolate bar, you'd think twice about sharing it with someone else, or sticking it up your bum like my mate Paul did when he had to spend a week in Doncaster jail.

The smartphone totally changed the way we ignore people. In previous centuries we might have ignored them by looking at a spinning jenny or putting mud in our eyes; now we ignored them by looking at our phones, tinkering with social media and getting polarised.

Smartphones have become part of our culture: it's commonplace now to see morons walk down the street without looking where they're going because they're staring at their screens. You're probably reading this on a phone now, walking out in front of a bus. I hope it hits you.

SOCIAL MEDIA

Thanks to being online all the time, you could fill in the gaps in your conversations with friends, family and the people serving you from behind counters in shops and bars by looking at your iPhone to see who was kicking off with who, what your ex looked like now, or what literally everyone was eating.

Social media was very much the internet of its day, a new communication arena where all the great debates of the twenty-first century took place. On social media you could ask: what was the best path from Britain in the twenty-first century? How can you remove a red-wine stain from a carpet? Is Ross Kemp a prick? Or all right actually? Asking for a friend.

THE GLOBAL GLOBE

The first of the social media networks was Facebook.*
Facebook was started up by some nerdy college blokes so
that other nerdy college blokes could wank-rate the female
students. But 'Wankratebook' turned out to be a terrible
name, so they made it all polite and pretended they were
looking at the girls' eyes or noses or something.

To begin with, Facebook was all harmless stuff, like 'I
remember you: I was at school with your brother', or 'That
bloke at number 55 looks like a wrong'un – let's burn his
house down just in case'. But then it turned nasty.

Political groups infected the place with proper gander.
Russia started posting things that made people vote for
baddies. The world was overwhelmed with This One Weird
Tips. Facebook had become an evil hypnotist, like Paul
McKenna but with a legally watertight accusation against
him which I've been told to point out I don't have.

Luckily, Twitter came along. Twitter was lovely, because
all the posts were so short that no one could write anything
horrible. But then people worked out how to make horrible
things short, and the whole thing sadly went to shit again.

And then, Twitter got shitter.

Twitter used to be run by someone called Jack who had
only one name, like Madonna or Paddington. But then Elon
Musk, who's a cross between Adolf Hitler and Willy Wonka,
accidentally bought it and accidentally made it worse and
worse and worse by accidentally bringing banned racists

---

* It wasn't, but no one remembers MySpace. I have asked on Reddit.

and weirdos back on board and accidentally posting bigoted and horrible things himself, and then accidentally renaming it and replacing its nice bird-in-a-blue-sky logo with something that looks like a piece of burning torture equipment. But then, accidents will happen.

Instagram is the only reliable place to find out what literally everyone is eating or what your ex looks like now. And the answer to both is: smashed avocado.

People eventually put their whole lives online, while ignoring people around them. If you weren't looking at what people were up to on Snapchat, then you might as well be dead. If it didn't happen in social media, it didn't happen.

BILLIONAIRES

Some people say that nobody needs a billion dollars, because it's impossible to ever spend that much money. But twenty-first-century billionaires have inspired us all by finding amazing new ways to waste more money than humans have ever done before, doing even more pointless things. It makes you proud to be human.

Inspired by the huge amount of money that NASA wasted pretending to go to the moon, billionaires like Elton Musk are planning to go to places that even fewer people want to go to – whether that's far-away horrible places like Mars, or shitty nobody's-impressed places like not-quite-as-far-as-the-moon-and-then-coming-straight-home-because-there's-fuck-all-up-there-apart-from-other-billionaires.

Going to space is great because the money of billionaires like Elton Musk would otherwise only be wasted on making earth better, and we know what that's like already: it's what it was like before billionaires like Elton Musk. Why go backwards to the olden days, when you can go forwards? Billionaires who spend their money on things on earth are boring. Like the Microsoft paperclip Bill Gates, who spent all the money he got for knowing you looked like you were writing a letter on getting rid of mosquitoes. He spent billions on that and a) you can do that with a rolled-up newspaper and b) there are still mosquitoes, so that proves it's better to go to Mars. Where there are already no mosquitoes, because nothing can survive there. (Scientists tell us the chances of anything coming from Mars are a million to one, and that's been proved by several successful stage versions.)

The billionaires won't be the first human things on Mars. We've sent robots to Mars before and they didn't complain, for the short time they lasted before they died in the awful conditions on the solar system's nearest dead Hell Planet that hates us. If robots love it on our neighbouring lonely red rock, surely the next people who will 100 per cent enjoy going there would be bored, rich white men with no friends. It's their dream holiday.

It's going to be great when the billionaires land, showing off that they'd got there before all the hotels and tourists spoiled it, and posting Instagram pictures of their hot-dog legs on the red sand beach – 'today's office ... LOL!' Spending billions on giving us all cosmic FOMO is a better use of their hard-earned money than saving the earth, and helping people they've never met, some of whom might be arseholes. I completely get why they're going. It looks brilliant. At least as good as Faliraki. But with less of a queue at check-in.

Post-Communist Russia: Yeltsin, Putin and the Ukraine

At the end of communism* Russia decided to go totally the other way, and go super-capitalist, like when your mum went from watching TV every night eating creme eggs for twenty years to going to swingers' parties every night for six months after her divorce from Dad. Yes, *your* mum. And what she was doing was really disgusting, I mean *really* disgusting. None of which I can go into in detail in a book that's meant to be a general history for the general reader twelve plus.

But the bits of capitalism Russia really got into were the two bits that Western capitalists try not to make too much of a big deal of: the corruption and the starvation.

After the fall of communism, the Russian government

---

* I've forgotten that I never finished telling you about Russia, which is a mistake because around the time of the invention of woke, they started having history again too. But to explain that, I have to go back to the end of when communism finished there, which was around the time the first series of *Baywatch Nights* aired, to give you some context.

gave everyone a share in the factories and industries they worked in, like John Lewis does. They thought that by giving everyone a share they'd all be rich, but in fact the very opposite happened, and soon everyone in Russia was poor, apart from a few corrupt men who bought all the shares from the poor starving Russians. They called these men Oily-gachs because they bought all the oil. Gach means something too, in Russian.

But the average man in the street couldn't afford a loaf of Russian bread, never mind a petrochemical complex in downtown Siberia. This wasn't the capitalism they'd seen in the movies on the bootlegged VHSs their cousin had smuggled in through Istanbul hidden in a pair of Levi 501s.

And to make matters worse, the Russian President wasn't like a president from the movies either. He was called Boris Yeltsin, who was a sort of enchanted drunk bear. The people liked him because he liked drinking and dancing like a proper Russian, not scheming and killing people like other proper Russians.

But the party could only last so long. And after the party comes the reckoning, as your mum found out after that sex party in Faversham. By 2000 Yeltsin had been replaced by a more traditional scheming, killing-people Russian, Vladimir Putin, the most frightening, Russianest, maddest Putin the world had seen since Ra Ra Rasputin. He was just what the people wanted after the poverty of the Yeltsin era: he was a strongman, a wrongman, a hard case and a nut job – like that bloke with the pencil moustache your mum started seeing after all the sex parties.

But unlike that man, who she left after six months because she realised he was an arsehole and had rules about how to fill a dishwasher, Putin moved fast to consolidate his power. He got the oligarchs in line and showed he was mental enough to do anything by drowning his own sailors on the *Kursk* submarine, and invading bits of Russia that were already Russian, like Chechnya. If he was mad enough to do that to his own people, what would he do to people who weren't? Or people who said they weren't but who he said were: the Ukrainians?

Ukraine was a bit of the old Soviet Union that was very happy not being Russia. But Putin said, no, you're transitioning to Russian, whether you like it or not. So he invaded Ukraine, and at the time of writing, he's invading it still.

Hope your mum's well.

History of Now

As history reaches today, deciding what is history and what isn't can be tricky, especially since there are no history books to help me, and even ChatGPT only knows up to January 2022. We're too close to events to know what is significant. For example, in one hundred years' time, what will historians think most worthy of recurring in their history books covering the twenty-first century – President

Trump's failed insurrection of 6 January 2021? Or the release of *Prince of Persia: The Lost Crown* on Nintendo Switch, PlayStation 4, PlayStation 5 Windows, Xbox One and Xbox Series X/S on 18 January 2024? Without the distance of time, it is impossible to know.

Even as I write these last few words of this book, war rages in the Holy Land. It's a conflict that is very hard to explain succinctly. So I won't bother. Hopefully both sides will see eye-to-eye and tooth-to-tooth soon. But not so soon that this final chapter is made out of date before publication. I think it'll be okay. Whatever. I've got a plane to catch.

2024

It turns out that 2024 is a terrible year to release a history book that goes up to modern times because so much is happening between April 2024 when this book has to be written by, and Christmas 2024 when it will be released to the world – elections, wars, new iPhones, *Love Island: All Stars* – that this page will go out of date very quickly.

God knows what happens to a book between April and Christmas – why that gap has to be so long – but I'm assured that this really does have to be finished by the end of April. With its slow turnaround and boring words, publishing is very much not the internet of its day.

Over half the world's population will vote in elections in

2024, and that will include me if I can't think of anything better to do, meaning that it would be pointless writing about who's in charge as of now. And with so much AI, alternative realities, echo chamber, simulations and misinformation around, no two people are going to have the same conception of the truth anyway. So you'll just have to fill in the rest of the history yourself on the next page. (I might update for the paperback if something really *juicy* happens in world history.)

THE GLOBAL GLOBE

In my reality of the world in [INSERT DATE HERE], this is what's happening . . .

> **IMMERSIVE HISTORY: THE TWENTY-FIRST CENTURY**
>
> 1. Go about your normal life: you're already immersed in the twenty-first century.

Mankind's Ultimate Achievement

As we reach the end of this history of the planet's history, it's fitting that we should take a moment to pause and contemplate the history of man's progress on earth – and then stop pausing to ask some pertainment questions: what is it all for? What does it all mean? Where has it all been leading? Have I written 50,000 words yet? *Almost. But not quite.* Four more. And then another two more.

What's it all about? It's a question that has been baffling philosophers, politicians and religious nuts ever since mankind learned to walk on his hind legs and shit in another room.

But now, in this book/podcast, I can exclusively reveal the answer. What's it all about? It's about this: the Synetech CN12 Colour All-In-One Inkjet Printer, Copier, Scanner and Fax.

It really is a wonderful machine. It connects simply to your computer using wi-fi and it couldn't be easier to use. Double-sided printing is a doddle, with the intuitive interface allowing you to change the settings as required. And it's a speedy mover – it can print up to twenty-two pages a minute in black and white, or up to twenty in colour. And it's very quiet: it's only fifty decibels when printing – meaning you can keep working, or not working, while it does its job.

Incredible. The colour is amazing. So life-like. If this book wasn't black and white only at the publisher's request we could show you how stunning its colours are.

You can also use the Synetech CN12 as a fax, scanner and copier, meaning this one little box can handle anything you might throw at it in the modern home-office environment. And Synetech's TruInkPlus ink delivery system means you'll never get a smudged or blurred print. Amazing.

As well as printing, faxing, scanning and copying, the Synetech CN12 has a host of other functions. For example, a couple of touches on the screen and – it dispenses a portion of just-toasted pine nuts. Delicious. And perfect for pesto, or whatever else you can do with pine nuts.

And unlike other printers, you don't have to worry if it gets haunted. Synetech exorcists are online twenty-four hours a day via the Synetech app.

They'll simply talk the spirit into leaving the printer, so you can enjoy more hassle-free printing, faxing, copying, pine-nutting and scanning. And even more amazing than that, the ink cartridges are reasonably priced too.

That's the Synetech CN12 – humankind's finest achievement.

To order a Synetech CN12 scan this QR Code.

Index

History, World, Philomena
    Cunk's recounting of, 1-244

Index, 245